SKILL SHARPENERS
Critical Thinking
Grade 2

The following illustrations were created by the artists listed (provided through AdobeStock.com) and are protected by copyright: photosvac (page 11); Alexey Bannykh (page 19)

The following illustrations were created by the artists listed (provided through Shutterstock.com) and are protected by copyright: Rich Carey, WeStudio (page 8); chloe7992, JIANG HONGYAN (page 9); KITSANANAN (page 10); Smit (page 11); Lilu330 (page 12); Mumut, Simple Concept (page 13); arbit (pages 16, 115, 116); BlueRingMedia (pages 14, 56); Jon Larter (page 18); vadimmmus (page 19); AlexanderZam (page 24); Protasov AN, Igor Chernomorchenko, Pan Xunbin, Panaiotidi (page 28); Afanasia, paul diaconu (page 29); Marina Sterina (page 30); Daniela Barreto (page 31); Matthew Cole (pages 32, 57, 74, 75, 102, 119); Linda Brotkorb (page 32); NikP (page 34); Christos Georghiou (page 35); Worraket (page 37); Teguh Mujiono (pages 37, 89, 105); pixelparticle (page 38); Lera Efremova (page 45); Rawpixel.com (page 46); art_of_sun, pichayasri, SKARIDA (page 47); Spreadthesign (pages 47, 96); Lorelyn Medina (pages 47, 75, 101, 105); Margarita Vodopyanova (page 52); Thodoris Tibilis (page 54); Andrei Zhukov (page 55); Juliar Studio, Lyudmyla Kharlamova (page 55); My Pet Dinosaur, NotionPic, Reshetnyova Oxana (page 57); Guryanov Andrey, iofoto (page 62); Nomad_Soul (page 63); Dimedrol68 (page 64); Motimo (page 65); Katrina.Happy (page 66); chotwit piyapramote (page 67); Mega Pixel, Samuel Acosta, Vereshchagin Dmitry (page 69); KennyK (page 72); Rawpixel.com (page 73); Digital Genetics (page 75); Maxx-Studio, Slavoljub Pantelic, vectorgirl (page 75); Africa Studio, Antiqva, GoodMood Photo, Nicolesa, Preto Perola (page 78); DenStudio, kuzzie (page 82); ANURAK PONGPATIMET (page 83); Anteromite, La Gorda, trekandshoot (page 84); Earto, Monkey Business Images, Olga1818 (page 85); StockSmartStart (page 87); stockakia (page 88); ekler (page 89); Iryna Dobrovynska (page 93); Hoika Mikhail, Kiselev Andrey Valerevich (page 94); espies, Inspiring, Pagina (page 95); harikarn, Vasilyeva Larisa (page 97); graphic-line (page 98); x7vector (page 99); Mathee saengkaew (page 100); ang intaravichian (page 101); HitToon (page 104); Azuzl, Memo Angeles, Sarawut Padungkwan, wong sze yuen (page 105); NORUEN (page 111); Quick Shot, Proskurina Yuliya (page 112); svaga (pages 113, 118); NEILRAS (page 113); Danilo Sanino (pages 114, 115); Feaspb (page 114); alexcoolok (page 115); Kauriana (page 117); jehsomwang (page 118); maritime_m (page 123); sumikophoto, Anton Foltin, Yavuz Sariyildiz (page 124); caramelina, Malchev (page 125); Robles Designery (page 127); larryrains, MSSA (page 128); CoSveta (page 129); Lokichen (page 130); graphixmania (page 131); SlipFloat (page 132)

Editorial Development: Rachel Lynette
Lisa Vitarisi Mathews
Jo Ellen Moore
Copy Editing: Laurie Gibson
Laurie Westrich
Art Direction: Yuki Meyer
Design/Production: Jessica Onken
Yuki Meyer

EMC 3252

Evan-Moor
Helping Children Learn

Visit
teaching-standards.com
to view a correlation
of this book.
This is a free service.

**Correlated to
Current Standards**

**Congratulations on your purchase of some of the
finest teaching materials in the world.**

EVAN-MOOR CORP.
phone 1-800-777-4362, fax 1-800-777-4332.
Entire contents © 2017 EVAN-MOOR CORP.
18 Lower Ragsdale Drive, Monterey, CA 93940-5746. Printed in China.

CPSIA: Asia Pacific Offset Ltd, Kowloon, Hong Kong [5/2019]

Contents

Things

Places

Practicing Critical Thinking Skills

Critical thinking comes naturally to young children. They learn autonomy through exploration, observe their environment using logic and reasoning, try new things, and think creatively. As children grow and enter an academic setting, some of the natural curiosity and problem-solving instincts are not engaged as often as they could be. This practice book encourages children to "think about their thinking" through creative, analytical, and evaluative tasks.

Read All About It

Have your child read the selection to you. Discuss how the illustrations and photos help your child better understand the topic. After reading the selection, discuss how the topic relates to your child's life.

Tell What You Know

The activities on these pages provide opportunities for children to connect their knowledge and opinions to the topic. Encourage your child to think about his or her experiences and support his or her curiosity by discussing the questions and topics together.

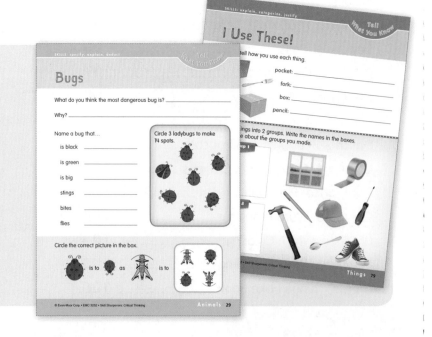

Critical Thinking Activities

The critical thinking activities are designed to engage children in application, analytical, synthesis, and evaluative tasks. The cross-curricular activities present science, math, social studies, and language arts content.

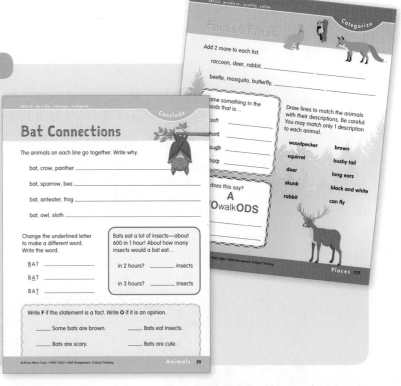

Art Projects and Hands-on Activities

The art projects and hands-on activities provide children with opportunities to use critical thinking skills to create. Encourage your child to tap into his or her creativity and innovation and to have fun with the hands-on activities. After your child completes each project, discuss the steps taken to create it. Encourage your child to explain what he or she enjoyed most and why.

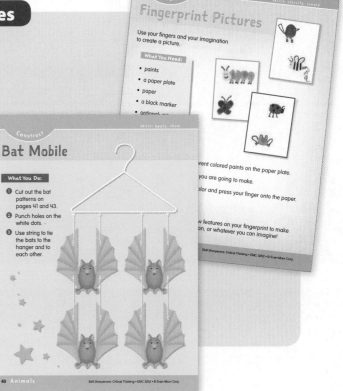

6

Alligators and Turtles

☑ I Did It! Check each activity as you complete it.

Be on the Lookout!

How many different turtles can you find on pages 8–13?

Count them and write the number here: _____

Facts About Alligators and Turtles

Read about alligators and turtles, then answer the questions on the following pages.

What has 4 legs, a backbone, and scales? If you guessed a turtle or an alligator, you are correct! Even though they look very different, both belong to a group called **reptiles**. All reptiles have scales.

An alligator has a long snout with strong jaws and sharp teeth. Its nostrils are near the top of the snout so it can breathe while hiding under water. An alligator is carnivorous, or meat-eating. It catches prey in its strong jaws. Small prey such as fish or birds is swallowed whole. It tears off pieces of big prey such as deer using its sharp teeth. An alligator can move very fast on land and in the water.

sea turtle

land turtle

There are many kinds of turtles. All turtles have tails. Turtles living in the ocean have flippers for swimming. Land turtles have round, stumpy legs for walking. They move slowly because of their heavy shells. The shell protects a turtle. It has a top and bottom and is connected on the sides. A turtle cannot crawl out of its shell. A turtle doesn't have teeth. It has a hard beak and jaws with hard ridges to cut and chew its food.

Both turtles and alligators lay eggs in nests. A female turtle digs a hole in dirt or sand and lays many eggs. A female alligator lays eggs in a nest made of plants.

Skill Sharpeners: Critical Thinking • EMC 3252 • © Evan-Moor Corp.

Alligators

Write 2 sentences about alligators.

1. An alligator _____.

2. _____ alligator.

Write **F** if the statement is a fact.
Write **O** if it is an opinion.

_____ Alligators have sharp teeth.

_____ Alligators are reptiles.

_____ Alligators are too big.

_____ Alligators can swim.

Can you think of 4 other animals with sharp teeth?

1. _____

2. _____

3. _____

4. _____

Draw an alligator with a bunny tail and bunny ears.

Turtles

What is a problem you might have if you had a shell like a turtle?

_____

_____

When would it be a **good** thing to have a shell like a turtle?

_____

_____

Which turtle is different?
Circle it.

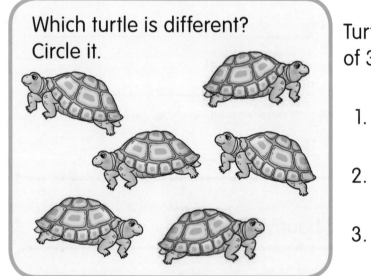

Turtles have shells. Can you think
of 3 other animals that have shells?

1. _____

2. _____

3. _____

Would you like to have a turtle for a pet? _____

Why or why not? _____

Alligators and Turtles

Read each numbered item. Does it tell about alligators, turtles, or both? Write the number in the Venn diagram. Then make up 2 of your own and write the numbers in the diagram.

Alligators

Turtles

Both

1. is a reptile

2. lives in the wild

3. has sharp teeth

4. has a tail

5. has a snout

6. has scales

7. has a shell

8. moves slowly

9. can swim

10. _____

11. _____

Compute

Word Problems

There were 17 sea turtles walking across the beach. There were 12 sea turtles sliding into the water. How many sea turtles in all?

Work Space:

_____ sea turtles

A sea turtle swam after a group of crabs. There were 18 crabs in the group. The sea turtle ate 7 of the crabs.

How many crabs were left?

Work Space:

_____ crabs

There were 3 sea turtles. The first turtle ate 8 sea grass plants. The next turtle ate 5 shrimp. The last turtle ate 4 jellyfish.

How many plants, shrimp, and jellyfish did they eat in all?

Work Space:

_____ in all

Van saw 14 turtles at the zoo. $\frac{1}{2}$ of the turtles were in the water. How many turtles were not in the water?

Work Space:

_____ turtles

Snack Time!

Speedy eats crickets every day. This graph shows how many crickets Speedy ate last week.

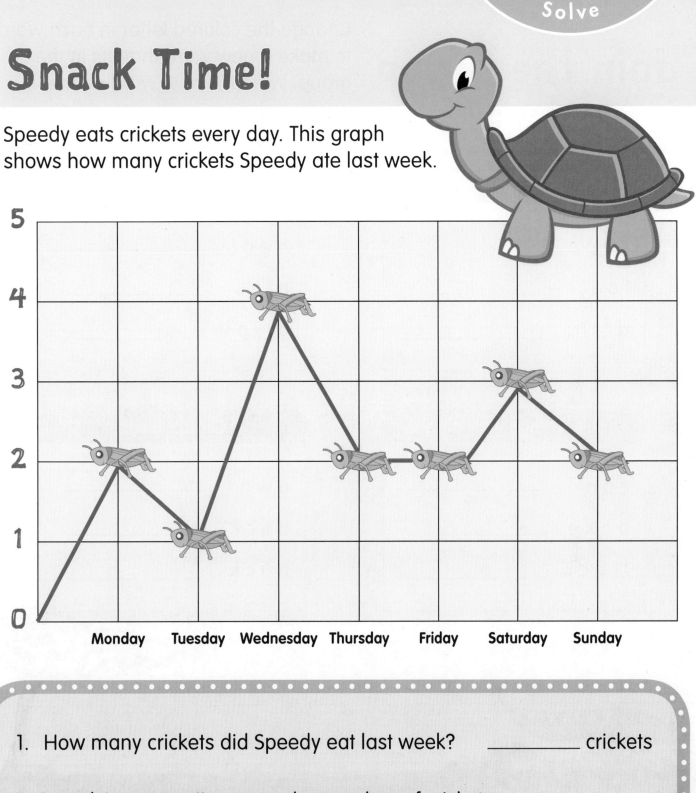

1. How many crickets did Speedy eat last week? _____ crickets

2. Speedy's owner, Jin, opened a new box of crickets last Monday. A box holds 30 crickets. How many crickets were left at the end of the week? _____ crickets

Convert

Join the Group

Change the colored letter in each word to make a new word that fits in the group. Write the new word on the line.

Group: Pets

c a p _____

l o g _____

d i s h _____

Group: Fruits

b e a r _____

p l u s _____

g r i p e _____

Group: Things with Wheels

c a n _____

b a k e _____

t r a c k _____

Group: Birds

o w n _____

d e c k _____

h a c k _____

Skill Sharpeners: Critical Thinking • EMC 3252 • © Evan-Moor Corp.

Draw

My Turtle

Follow the directions to draw a turtle.
Then color your turtle and answer the questions.

The turtle has a _____ on its back.

A turtle likes to nibble on _____.

A turtle moves so _____.

Animals

Produce

I Like Word Problems

Write word problems about this picture. Show how to find the answers.

Write an addition word problem.

Write a subtraction word problem.

Write a multiplication word problem.

Determine

It's Gator Time!

What do alligators eat?

_____

Write 3 words that describe alligators.

1. _____

2. _____

3. _____

An alligator has about 80 teeth. How many teeth do 2 alligators have?

_____ teeth

If an alligator lost 6 teeth, how many would it have left?

_____ teeth left

Which alligator is different? Circle it.

Find

Gator Words

The word **ALLIGATOR** appears 10 times in this word search.
Look across, up and down, and backwards.
Circle each word and cross off a number each time.

1   2   3   4   5   6   7   8   9   10

```
R B R O T A G I L L A
O A L L I G A T O R L
T L F P J U I E L Y L
A L L I G A T O R B I
G I C T D W M X O R G
I G R O T A G I L L A
L A L L I G A T O R T
L T K C N H Q Z V G O
A O A L L I G A T O R
S R O T A G I L L A D
```

Use the letters in **ALLIGATOR** to write new words.

_____   _____

_____   _____

_____   _____

Let's Talk Turtle

What animal is slower than a turtle? _____

Is an ant slower than a turtle? _____

Why or why not? _____

Write the missing numbers on the turtles.

Write **F** if the statement is a fact.
Write **O** if it is an opinion.

_____ Turtles have shells.

_____ Turtles are cute.

_____ Turtles make good pets.

_____ Turtles are reptiles.

How could you help this turtle without touching it with your hands?

_____

Design

An Unusual Shell

Use just 4 colors to color the spaces on the turtle's shell.
The spaces that are the same color must **not** touch each other.

Hint: Plan your design before you start to color.

Log Hop

Help the rabbit get to the other side of the river without being eaten by alligators. The rabbit can hop **only** on logs and must hop on exactly 16 logs. Color the logs the rabbit uses.

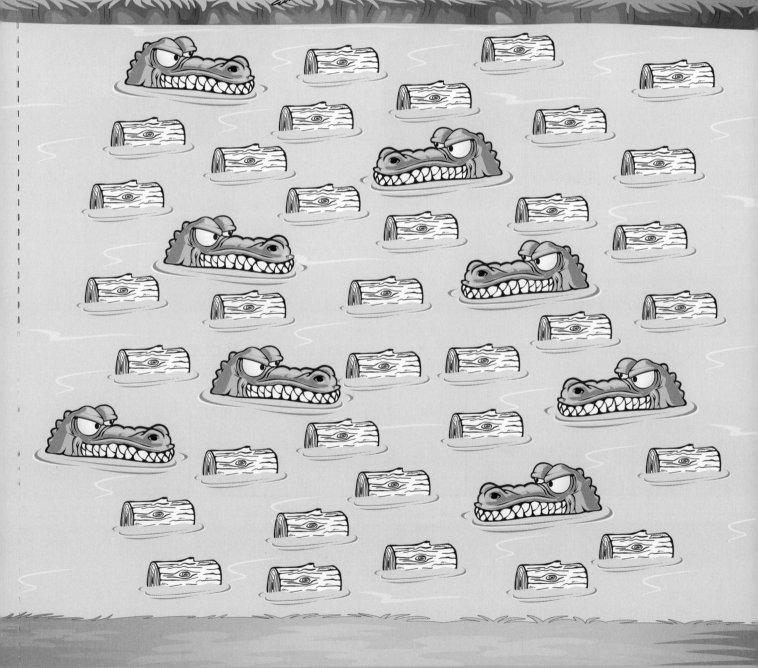

Animals   **21**

Create

Turtle Puppet

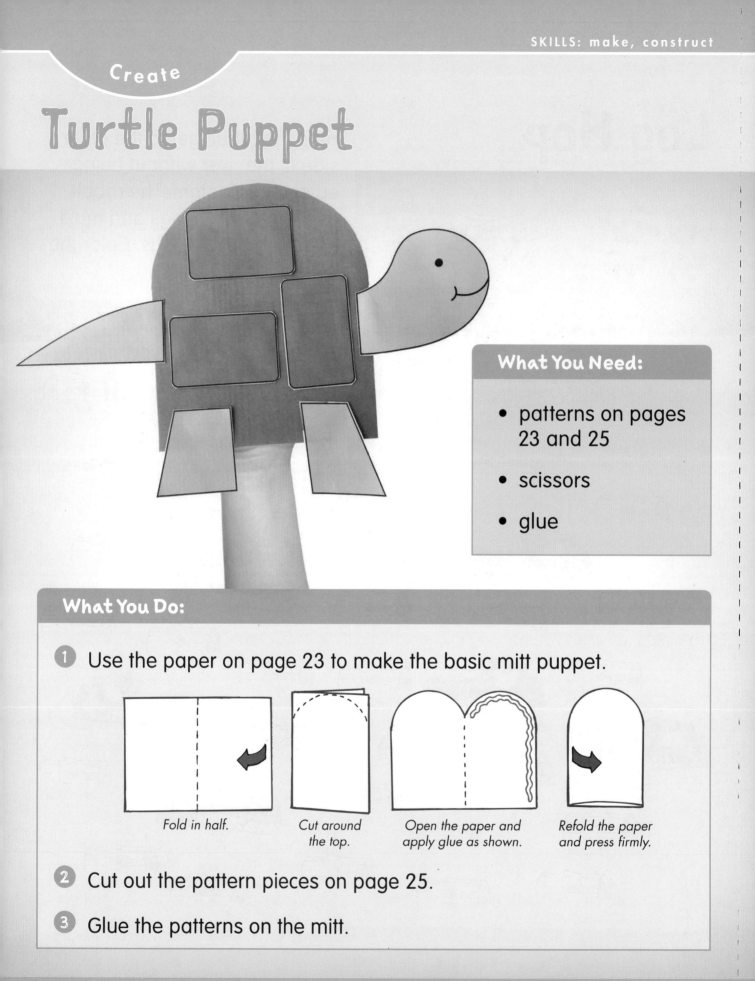

What You Need:

- patterns on pages 23 and 25
- scissors
- glue

What You Do:

1. Use the paper on page 23 to make the basic mitt puppet.

Fold in half.   *Cut around the top.*   *Open the paper and apply glue as shown.*   *Refold the paper and press firmly.*

2. Cut out the pattern pieces on page 25.

3. Glue the patterns on the mitt.

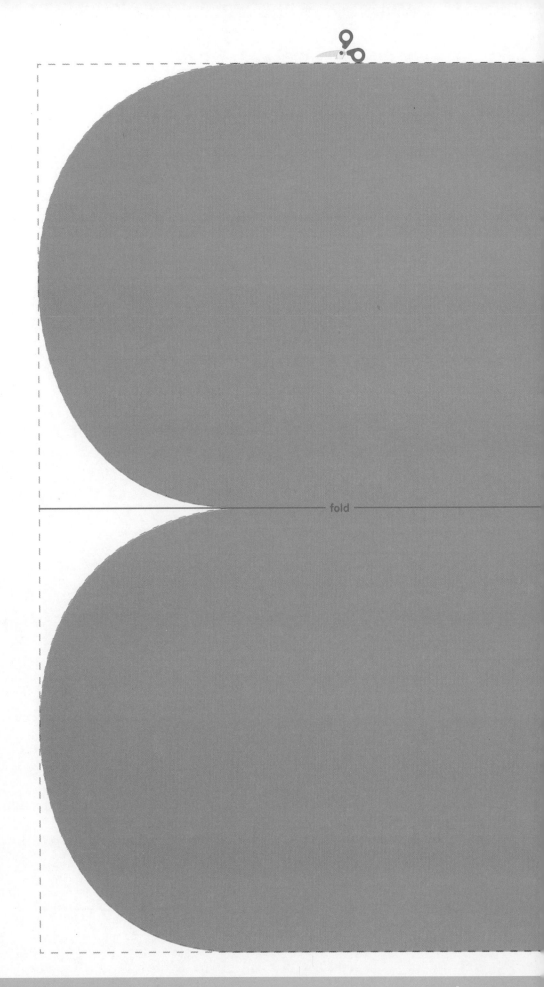

fold

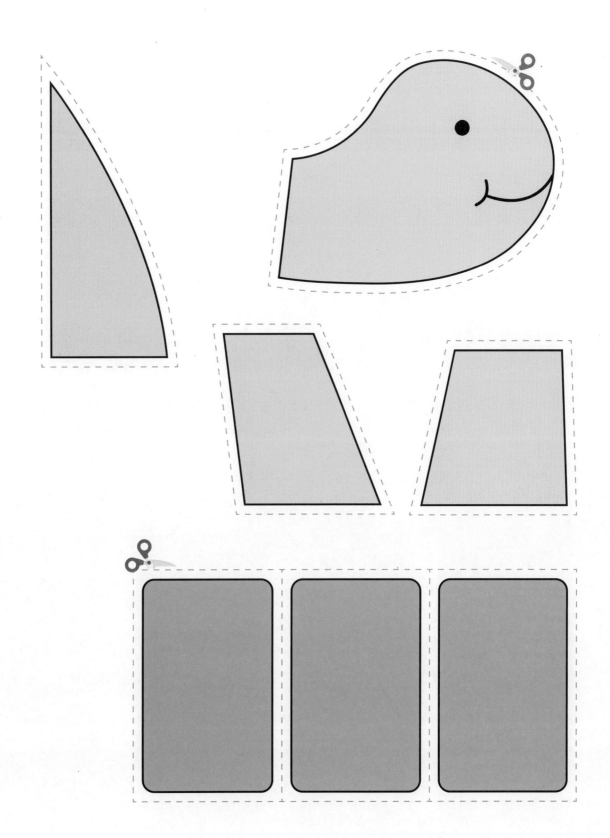

Bats and Bugs

☑ I Did It! Check each activity as you complete it.

Be on the Lookout!

How many different bugs can you find on pages 29–33?
Count them and write the number here: _____

Facts About Bats and Bugs

Read about bats and bugs, then answer the questions on the following pages.

Imagine having wings instead of arms. And hanging upside down to sleep. There is only one mammal that can do this—the bat! Like other mammals, bats have live babies that are fed milk by their mothers. And the arms of a bat have been changed into wings.

Bats that find food in the dark use echolocation. They make sounds and listen for echoes to find their way around.

There are bats that eat fruit. Others eat insects. Some eat small fish or other animals. Some people are afraid of bats, but bats are helpful animals. Some bats pollinate plants or spread seeds as they eat.

Do you call ants, bees, and grasshoppers "bugs"? Many people call all insects bugs, but only some insects are true bugs. Whether you call them bugs or insects, they are alike in these ways:

- They all have 3 body parts, 6 legs, and 2 antennae.
- They also have an exoskeleton. This means their skeleton is on the outside.

Most bugs lay eggs. Most can fly. Some bugs are helpful. Honeybees pollinate flowers and make honey. Some bugs are harmful. Grasshoppers eat plants in gardens and fields. You must be careful around some bugs. Bees and wasps can sting you. Mosquitos and ants can bite you. Bugs and ants live in colonies and work together.

The next time you're in nature, look around and see if you can find any bats or bugs—you might learn more about them!

Skill Sharpeners: Critical Thinking • EMC 3252 • © Evan-Moor Corp.

Bugs

What do you think the most dangerous bug is? _____

Why? _____

Name a bug that...

is black   _____

is green   _____

is big   _____

stings   _____

bites   _____

flies   _____

Circle 3 ladybugs to make 14 spots.

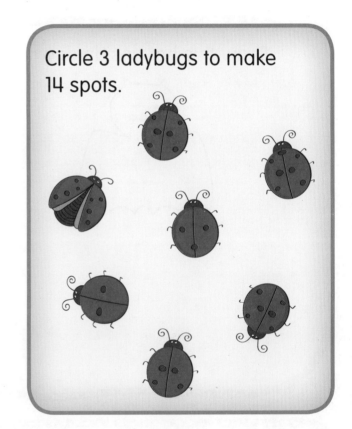

Circle the correct picture in the box.

is to   as   is to

Bats

Are you afraid of bats? _____

Why or why not? _____

Draw this bat upside down.

What words rhyme with **bat**?

_____

_____

_____

_____

_____

_____

How many insects did each bat eat? Write the number.

5   3   6   4   2   2

7   6   3   5   4

Skill Sharpeners: Critical Thinking • EMC 3252 • © Evan-Moor Corp.

Bug Match

Find the matching bugs and color them the same. One pair are **not** bugs! Circle them.

Compute

Cave

Benjamin Bat flew exactly 20 miles to get back to his cave. Trace the lines to show his path. Each number shows how many miles.

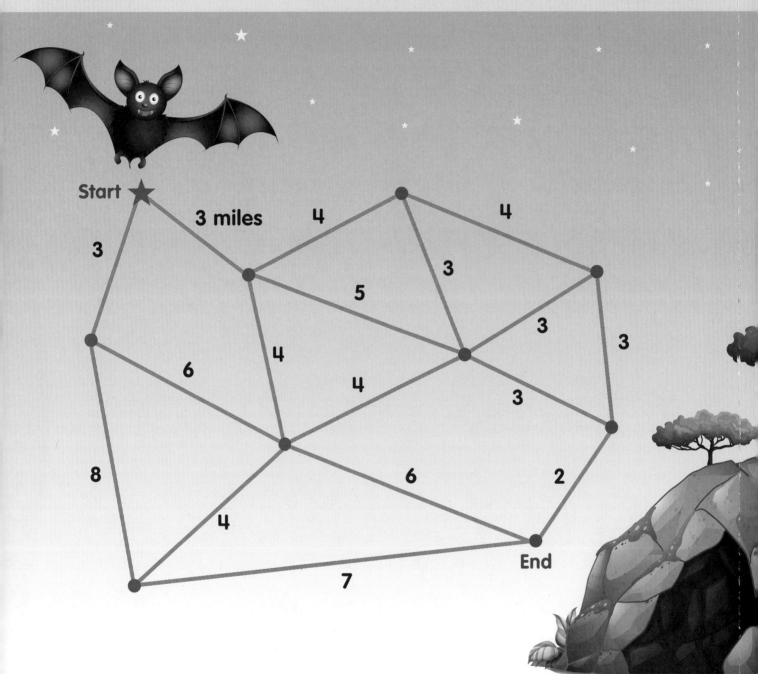

Write the equation that equals 20.

_____

Skill Sharpeners: Critical Thinking • EMC 3252 • © Evan-Moor Corp.

Compute

Word Problems

A line of ants was crawling on and around Stan's sandwich. "I'll bet there are 325 ants on my sandwich," said Stan. "And there must be 550 ants coming in a line."

How many ants did Stan guess there were in all?

Work Space:

_____ ants

Stan, Fran, and Dan saw a spider catch a fly in its web.

If the spider ate 6 flies every day, how many flies would it eat in a week?

Work Space:

_____ flies

Stan, Fran, and Dan went on an insect hunt in the backyard. They saw 24 ladybugs, 11 butterflies, 3 grasshoppers, and 13 ants.

How many insects did they see in all?

Work Space:

_____ insects

Pretend that a spider and a fly were wearing shoes.

1. How many shoes would they need in all?
2. How many **pairs** of shoes would they need?

Work Space:

_____ shoes

_____ pairs of shoes

Find

Hidden Animals

Caves are home to many animals. Unscramble the animal names below. Then find the animals in the cave and color them.

orgf _____   tab _____   tra _____

hifs _____   prised _____   tickerc _____

Odd Animal Out

Circle the animal that does **not** belong. Then tell why.

1. turtle   lizard   fox   rattlesnake

_____

2. cow   pig   chicken   tiger

_____

3. cub   camel   kitten   joey

_____

4. squirrel   honeybee   bat   bird

_____

5. walrus   lion   penguin   seal

_____

6. beetle   ladybug   cricket   spider

_____

7. bear   shark   whale   octopus

_____

Three of the animal names above are compound words.
Write them on the lines below.

_____ _____ _____

Solve

Bug Clues

Write a sentence about moths. Use exactly 6 words.

_____

Draw the other half of each bug.

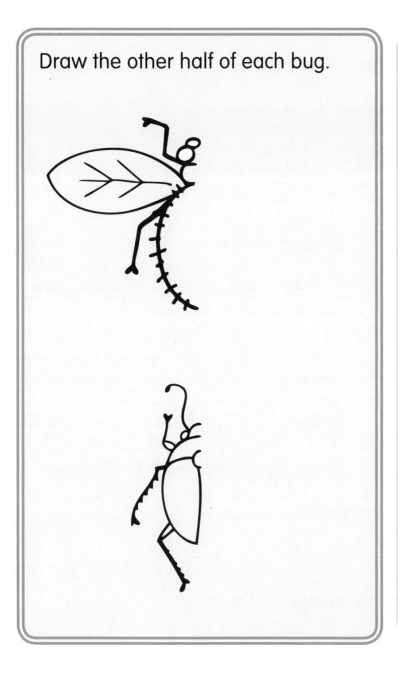

I am red with black spots. What bug am I?

_____

I make a chirping sound. What bug am I?

_____

I can live on a dog or on a cat. What bug am I?

_____

I live in a colony with a queen. What bug am I?

_____

Skill Sharpeners: Critical Thinking • EMC 3252 • © Evan-Moor Corp.

Cave Maze

Find your way through the cave maze.

Solve

Who Am I?

Use the code to name each bat.

I am the largest bat. I have a wingspan of 6 feet (1.8 m). Who am I?

	a	b	c	d	e
1	A	B	E	F	G
2	I	L	M	N	O
3	P	R	T	U	V
4	X	Y			

___ ___ ___ ___ ___ ___
1d   2b   4b   2a   2d   1e

___ ___ ___
1d   2e   4a

I am the smallest bat. I weigh less than a penny. Who am I?

___ ___ ___ ___ ___ ___ ___ ___ ___
1b   3d   2c   1b   2b   1c   1b   1c   1c

___ ___ ___
1b   1a   3c

I am the bat that eats blood. Who am I?

___ ___ ___ ___ ___ ___ ___
3e   1a   2c   3a   2a   3b   1c

___ ___ ___
1b   1a   3c

Skill Sharpeners: Critical Thinking • EMC 3252 • © Evan-Moor Corp.

Conclude

Bat Connections

The animals on each line go together. Write why.

bat, crow, panther _____

bat, sparrow, bee _____

bat, anteater, frog _____

bat, owl, sloth _____

Change the underlined letter to make a different word. Write the word.

BAT _____

B**A**T _____

BA**T** _____

Bats eat a lot of insects—about 600 in 1 hour! About how many insects would a bat eat…

in 2 hours? _____ insects

in 3 hours? _____ insects

Write **F** if the statement is a fact. Write **O** if it is an opinion.

_____ Some bats are brown.   _____ Bats eat insects.

_____ Bats are scary.   _____ Bats are cute.

Construct

Bat Mobile

What You Do:

1. Cut out the bat patterns on pages 41 and 43.

2. Punch holes on the white dots.

3. Use string to tie the bats to the hanger and to each other.

Skill Sharpeners: Critical Thinking • EMC 3252 • © Evan-Moor Corp.

Eyes, Teeth, and Hair

✓ I Did It! Check each activity as you complete it.

Be on the Lookout!

How many times can you find the word **eyes** on pages 47–55? Count them and write the number here: _____

Facts About Eyes, Teeth, and Hair

Read about eyes, teeth, and hair, then answer the questions on the following pages.

What do you see when you look in a mirror? There's your face looking back at you! What do you know about what you see?

First of all, you couldn't see anything if you didn't have eyes. We can see everything around us. We use our eyes to see the safest way to walk along a street. We use our eyes to find the things we need to use. You are using your sense of sight right now to read. Eyes can be many different colors—brown, blue, green, gray, or hazel. What color are your eyes?

If you are smiling when you look in the mirror, you will see your teeth. Teeth help us to bite and chew our food. It would be pretty difficult to swallow everything whole! We use our teeth to make some sounds when we talk. Say the word "see." Did you feel your teeth touch for the sound "s" makes? People have two sets of teeth as they grow. First you have your "baby" teeth. These fall out and a new set of teeth grow in. It is important to take care of your teeth. You need to brush, floss, and see the dentist to keep your teeth strong and healthy.

Touch the top of your head. What do you feel? Most people have hair on their heads. Hair may be short, long, or in between. Hair can be curly or straight. People have many different hair colors. Hair can be black, brown, blond, red, or gray. What color is your hair? Is it short or long?

Tell someone about your face. Describe your eyes, teeth, and hair.

My Eyes

What are 3 things that you **cannot** do with your eyes closed?

1. _____

2. _____

3. _____

What is something that you can do even when your eyes are closed?

_____

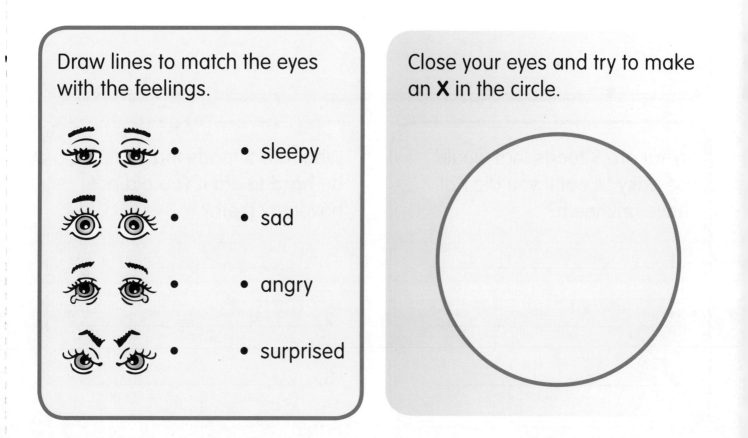

Draw lines to match the eyes with the feelings.

• • sleepy

• • sad

• • angry

• • surprised

Close your eyes and try to make an **X** in the circle.

Tell What You Know

My Teeth

How many teeth do you have? _____

How did you count them? _____

How many teeth are missing? _____

Draw your smile.

What are 3 foods that would be **easy** to eat if you did not have any teeth?

1. _____

2. _____

3. _____

What are 3 foods that would be **hard** to eat if you did not have any teeth?

1. _____

2. _____

3. _____

Skill Sharpeners: Critical Thinking • EMC 3252 • © Evan-Moor Corp.

My Hair

What are 3 things that you need to do to take care of your hair?

1. _____

2. _____

3. _____

Which one does not belong?

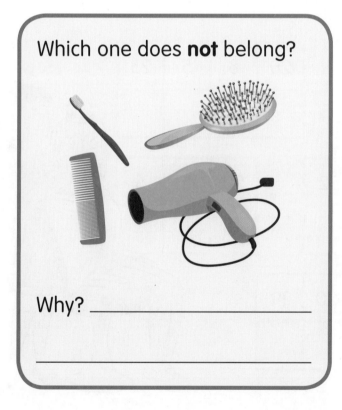

Why? _____

_____

Write 4 words that describe your hair.

1. _____

2. _____

3. _____

4. _____

Why doesn't it hurt to get your hair cut? _____

_____

Solve

A Hairy Riddle

Use the code to find the answer to the riddle.

1 A	2 B	3 C	4 D	5 E	6 F	7 G	8 H	9 I	10 J	11 K	12 L	13 M
14 N	15 O	16 P	17 Q	18 R	19 S	20 T	21 U	22 V	23 W	24 X	25 Y	26 Z

Why do barbers make good drivers?

2	5	3	1	21	19	5

20	8	5	25

11	14	15	23

1	12	12

20	8	5

19	8	15	18	20	3	21	20	19

Explain the answer to the riddle.

_____

_____

Skill Sharpeners: Critical Thinking • EMC 3252 • © Evan-Moor Corp.

My Face

Follow the directions to draw a face.
Then color your face and answer the questions.

My hair is _____.

My eyes are _____.

I look like my _____.

Describe

I See

Look at your eyes in a mirror.
Write each color you see.

_____

_____

_____

_____

How many eyes are
in your house right now?

_____ eyes

How many eyes belong to girls?

_____ eyes

How many eyes belong to boys?

_____ eyes

Look around you. What do you see in each of these directions? Draw it.

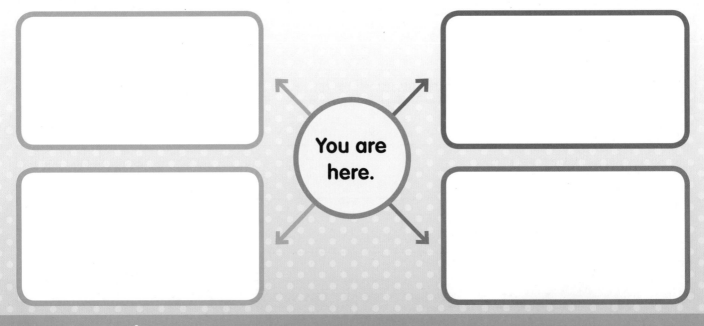

You are here.

Skill Sharpeners: Critical Thinking • EMC 3252 • © Evan-Moor Corp.

Compute

Word Problems

1. Kira's hair grows 3 inches (7.5 cm) every 6 months. Kira is getting a haircut today. Her hair is 12 inches (30 cm) long from her chin past her shoulders. She wants her hair to be only half that length. How much should she ask the hairdresser to cut off? _____

   How long will it take for Kira's hair to be 12 inches (30 cm) long again? _____

2. Jun is 7 years old. He has been losing 2 teeth every year since he was 4. How many teeth has he lost in all? _____

3. Lupe wants to know how many people in her class have green eyes. She made a graph of all of her classmates' eye colors. Count the tally marks to answer the questions.

   What is the answer to Lupe's question?

   _____

   What eye color do most students have?

   _____

   What eye color do the fewest students have?

   _____

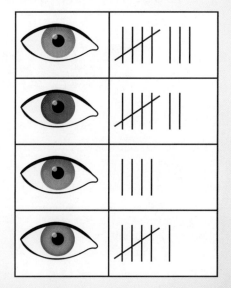

Add a tally mark to the chart to show what eye color you have.

My Body 53

Decide

Open Wide!

1. Circle the one that **cannot** be a **dentist**.

   a doctor   a man   a vet   a woman

2. Circle the word that rhymes with **tooth**.

   boo   booth   both   broth

3. Circle the word that does **not** belong.

   cast   cavity   tooth   pain

4. Circle the word that is a synonym for **ache**.

   ask   ear   ouch   pain

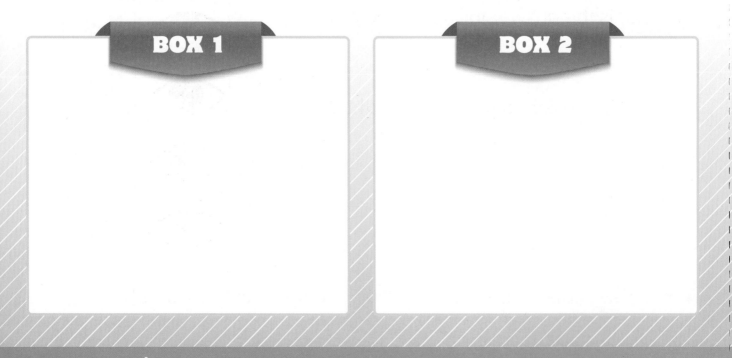

5. In Box 1, draw foods that are not good for your teeth. In Box 2, draw foods that are good for your teeth. Add labels that name each food.

   BOX 1

   BOX 2

What Is It?

Read the clue. Look at the pictures. Write the letter of the clue below the picture it tells about. Then write the word to solve the clue.

A. You hold it in your hand and use a downward motion to help you look tidy.

B. You hold it in your hand and use it with a cream to clean.

C. You use these to find out what is going on around you.

D. You have a lot of these, and they are always growing.

E. It is a thin string used to clean.

F. It washes the dirt out of your hair.

_____   _____   _____

_____   _____   _____

_____   _____   _____

_____   _____   _____

Deduce

The Answer Is...

Write the word for each clue. Then write the letters from the colored boxes to answer the riddle below.

What you put on your toothbrush

___ ___ ___ ___ ___ ___ ___ ___ ___ ___

A sweet food that is bad for your teeth

___ ___ ___ ___ ___

What you use to clean between your teeth

___ ___ ___ ___ ___

The pink area around your teeth

___ ___ ___ ___

What you use to clean your teeth

___ ___ ___ ___ ___ ___ ___ ___ ___

What has teeth but does not have a mouth?

☐ ☐ ☐ ☐ ☐

A Bird's-Eye View

Pretend that you have a bird's eyes.
Draw how each of these things would look if you were flying over them.

Apply
I See Colors!

The Northern Lights display a beautiful array of colors for our eyes to see. Use the color guide to color the Northern Lights.

Color Key

1 = orange   3 = violet   5 = red   7 = blue
2 = pink   4 = green   6 = black   8 = yellow

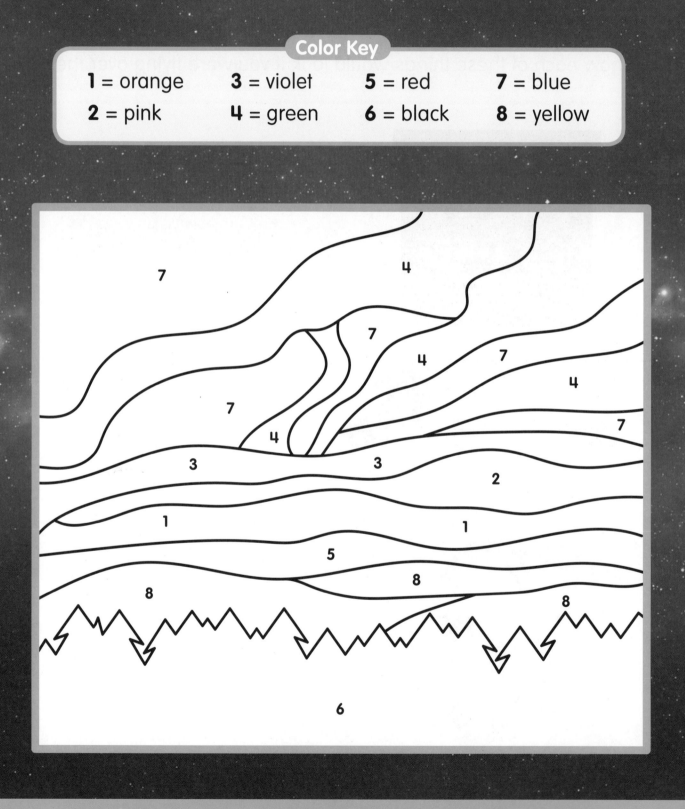

Skill Sharpeners: Critical Thinking • EMC 3252 • © Evan-Moor Corp.

Look at Me!

What You Need:

- a paper plate

- a pencil

- colored pencils, crayons, or markers

- glue

- yarn

What You Do:

1. Look in the mirror. Notice your eye color, your hair color, the shape of your nose, the shape of your mouth, and your other facial features.

2. Draw a picture of your face on the paper plate.

3. Color your picture to look like you.

4. Cut yarn to match your hair color and style. Glue it to the paper plate.

5. Use crafts to make the face look more like your own.

6. Show your picture to your family and ask if they can guess who it is!

Hands and Feet

✓ I Did It! Check each activity as you complete it.

Be on the Lookout!

How many times can you find the word **hands** on pages 63–69? Count and write the number here: _____

Facts About Hands and Feet

Read about hands and feet, then answer the questions on the following pages.

Every day your hands and feet work hard. They are used from the time you get up in the morning until you go to bed at night. Think about all they do.

Hands and fingers are used in many different ways. They hold a fork when you eat. They hold a pencil when you write. They tap letters on a keyboard when you type. Hands help you throw or catch a ball. They even scratch you when you get an itch! There is something special about each of your hands—the thumb. A thumb can work with your fingers to pinch, pick up, or hold on to things. Try to pick up a pencil without using your thumb. Can you do it?

Feet and toes work hard, too. Your feet hold your whole body up when you stand. Feet carry you from place to place. They help you to walk, run, skip, dance, and play. Imagine moving around without the help of your feet.

Your fingers and toes are called **digits**. How many digits do you have? That's right. You have 20. There are 10 on your hands and 10 on your feet. There are many bones in both your fingers and toes. Joints in each finger and toe allow you to bend them. Wiggle your fingers. Can you see how well each part moves? Now wiggle your toes. Do they move less or more than your fingers?

Skill Sharpeners: Critical Thinking • EMC 3252 • © Evan-Moor Corp.

My Hands

Imagine that you do not have hands.
How could you do each of these things?

write your name _____

play the piano _____

drink a cup of water _____

Write what each hand gesture means.

_____ _____ _____ _____

What are 3 words that rhyme with **hand**?

1. _____

2. _____

3. _____

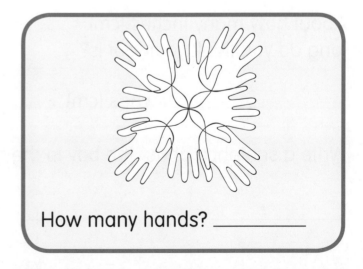

How many hands? _____

Tell What You Know

My Feet

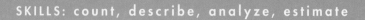

How many toes are in your house right now? _____

How many toes belong to girls? _____

How many toes belong to boys? _____

What are 4 words that describe your feet?

1. _____

2. _____

3. _____

4. _____

About how many inches (cm) long do you think your foot is?

_____ inches (cm)

What is wrong with this picture?

_____

Write a sentence about the boy in the picture.

_____

Terrific Toes

Read the poem. Then write to tell why you like it or why you don't.

> I have such terrific toes,
>
> I take them with me wherever I goes.
>
> I have such fantastic feet,
>
> No matter what, they still smell sweet.
>
> Toes and feet and feet and toes,
>
> There's nothing else as fine as those.
>
> –Anonymous

_____

_____

_____

Does the poem describe how you feel about your toes?

_____

Compare
Hand Shadows

It's fun to make animal shadows with your hands. Draw lines to match the hands, shadow, and name of the animal. Then get a friend and a flashlight and make some shadows yourself!

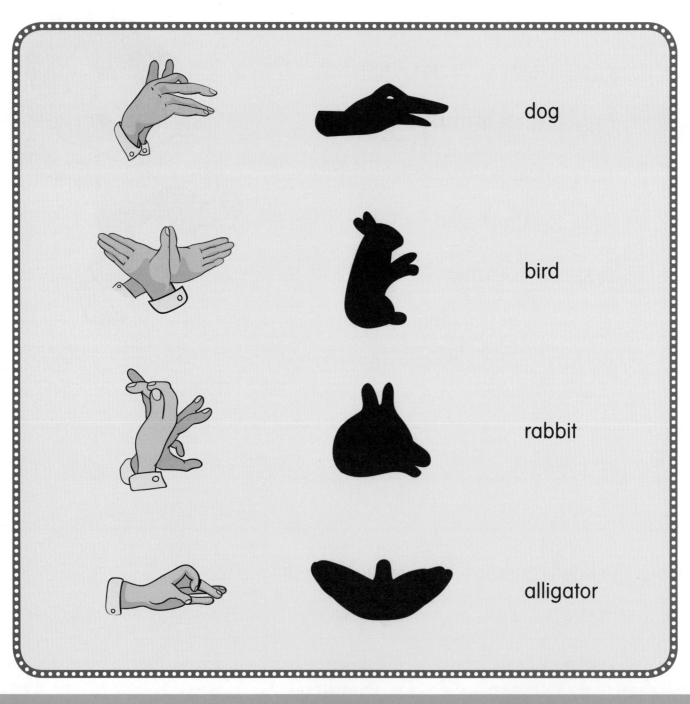

dog

bird

rabbit

alligator

Skill Sharpeners: Critical Thinking • EMC 3252 • © Evan-Moor Corp.

Deduce

Foot Notes

Foot goes with **sock** in the same way that **hand** goes with

_____.

Foot goes with **toes** in the same way that **hand** goes with

_____.

Unscramble these parts of a foot.

E L E H _____

O E T _____

L O E S _____

O E T L I N A _____

What do you wear on your feet when…

it is hot? _____

it is rainy? _____

it is nighttime? _____

they are cold? _____

What is something that you might put on your feet besides shoes or socks?

_____

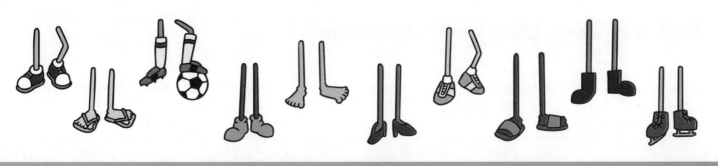

My Body 67

Find
A Handy Puzzle

Find the words in the word search. Check off each word you find. Words can go backwards, forwards, up and down, and diagonal.

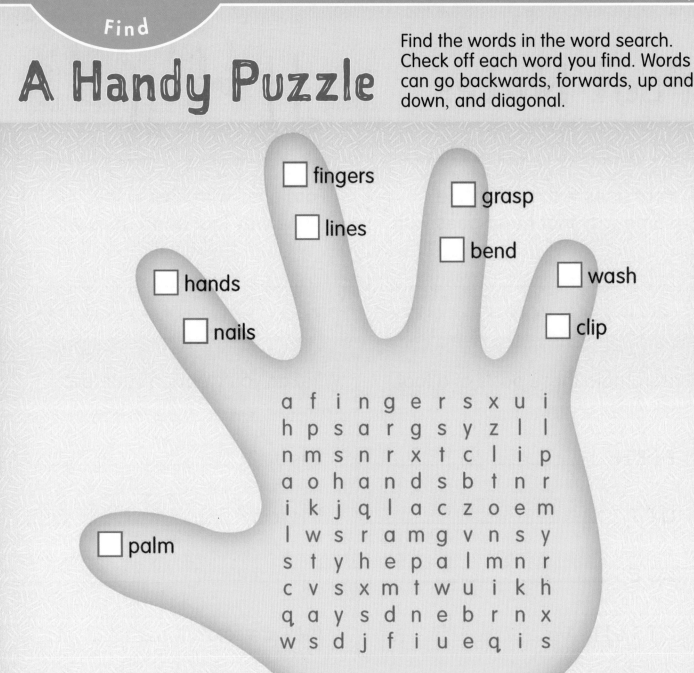

☐ fingers

☐ lines

☐ grasp

☐ bend

☐ hands

☐ nails

☐ wash

☐ clip

☐ palm

```
a f i n g e r s x u i
h p s a r g s y z l l
n m s n r x t c l i p
a o h a n d s b t n r
i k j q l a c z o e m
l w s r a m g v n s y
s t y h e p a l m n r
c v s x m t w u i k h
q a y s d n e b r n x
w s d j f i u e q i s
```

Write a sentence. Use 3 words from above.

_____

_____

Word Problems

Each boat has one pair of oars.
How many hands do you
need to hold the oars?

4 boats = [ ] oars = [ ] hands

9 boats = [ ] oars = [ ] hands

2 boats = [ ] oars = [ ] hands

6 boats = [ ] oars = [ ] hands

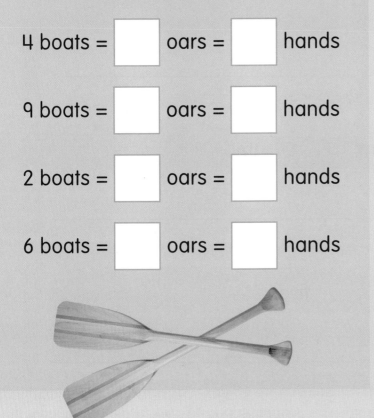

It costs $5.00 an hour to rent
a boat.

How much would it cost to
rent a boat for 2 hours?

$ [ ] for 2 hours

How much would it cost to
rent a boat for 4 hours?

$ [ ] for 4 hours

12 parents, 16 girls, and 22 boys rode to the lake on a bus.

How many people were there on the bus? [ ]

How many feet? [ ]

Justify

Connections

Three of the words in each row belong together.
Circle the word that does not belong.
Then write to explain why the three items are alike.

1. heel   nail   arch   stretch

_____

2. bend   kick   drink   jump

_____

3. ten   six   two   five

_____

4. clip   bend   file   scrub

_____

5. grasp   write   hop   hold

_____

Skill Sharpeners: Critical Thinking • EMC 3252 • © Evan-Moor Corp.

Footprints

Draw what Dylan did while he was at the beach. Be sure to draw his footprints.

- Dylan wrote his name in the sand near the beach blanket.
- Next, he decided to get ice cream.
- When he was done with his ice cream, he built a sand castle between the ice cream stand and the water.
- Then he went back to the beach blanket to get his little sister.
- Finally, Dylan and his sister ran into the water together!

Compute

Let's Play!

Mark needs his hands and feet to play baseball. He is a great batter. He has hit the ball in the last 6 games he played. He wants to get 30 hits this season.

Mark's Hits	
game 1	4 hits
game 2	2 hits
game 3	3 hits
game 4	1 hit
game 5	5 hits
game 6	3 hits

1. How many hits has Mark made so far? _____ hits

2. How many more does he need to make 30? _____ hits

3. Do you think Mark will make more or less hits next season? Why?

_____

_____

Hand Writings

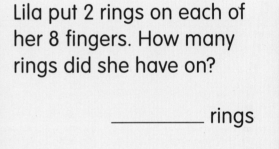

Compose

Finish the sentences in 2 different ways.

My hands _____.

My hands _____.

Fill in the missing vowels for these parts of your hand.

p _____ l m

f _____ n g _____ r s

k n _____ c k l _____ s

w r _____ s t

f _____ n g _____ r n _____ _____ l s

Lila put 2 rings on each of her 8 fingers. How many rings did she have on?

_____ rings

Then she took the rings off her pinkies. How many rings does she have on now?

_____ rings

What are 3 different ways you can warm your hands in the winter?

1. _____

2. _____

3. _____

My Body 73

Your Hand

Draw your hand in the box below. Include details. What shape are your nails? Where are the lines on your hand? Begin by tracing your hand.

Write a sentence that describes your hand.

_____

_____

Lost Shoes

Jill left her gym shoes somewhere. Help her find them. Draw a line to show Jill's path to her shoes.

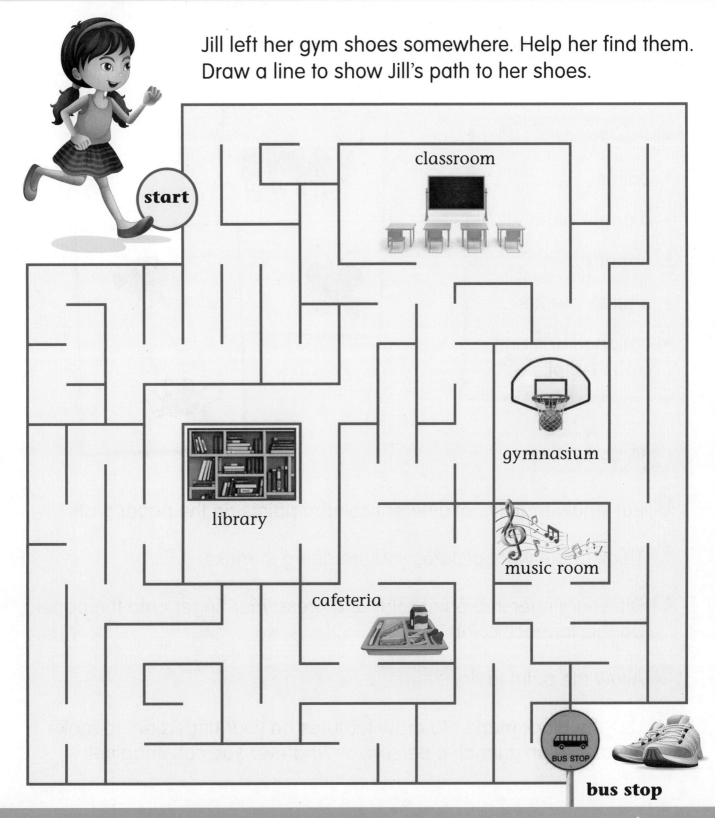

Create

Fingerprint Pictures

Use your fingers and your imagination to create a picture.

What You Need:

- paints
- a paper plate
- paper
- a black marker
- optional: arts and crafts supplies

What You Do:

1. Put small amounts of different colored paints on the paper plate.

2. Think about what pictures you are going to make.

3. Dip your finger in a paint color and press your finger onto the paper. Do this for each color.

4. Allow the paint to dry.

5. Use the black marker to draw features on your fingerprint to make it look like an animal, a person, or whatever you can imagine!

Skill Sharpeners: Critical Thinking • EMC 3252 • © Evan-Moor Corp.

Things We Use

✓ I Did It! Check each activity as you complete it.

Be on the Lookout!

How many tools can you find on pages 79–84?

Count them and write the number here: _____

Facts About Things We Use

Read about things we use, then answer the questions on the following pages.

Think about how many different things we use in our everyday lives. We use shoes, socks, hats, forks, spoons, tools, windows, doors, telephones, toothbrushes, pencils, paper—and the list goes on and on!

Do you ever wonder who invented the things you use? Or when they were invented? Or why they were invented? Most things are invented because of a need.

People needed to keep their feet warm.

People needed to protect their feet.

People needed light in their home. People wanted to see outside.

People needed to keep the cold air out of their home.

Some of the things we use are tools to help make work easier. For example, a toothbrush is a tool. A fork is a tool. A hammer is a tool. A pencil is a tool. Tools are used at home, at school, at work, and many other places, such as the doctor's office or the garden shop. What tools do you use?

People use some things so often that they may not know what to do without them. Many people have pockets in their clothes. They put money, keys, phones, pens, gum, and all kinds of things they use in their pockets. Some people use backpacks to hold the things they use. What things do you use every day? What would you do if you could not use them anymore?

I Use These!

Write to tell how you use each thing.

pocket: _____

fork: _____

box: _____

pencil: _____

Put these things into 2 groups. Write the names in the boxes.
Tell someone about the groups you made.

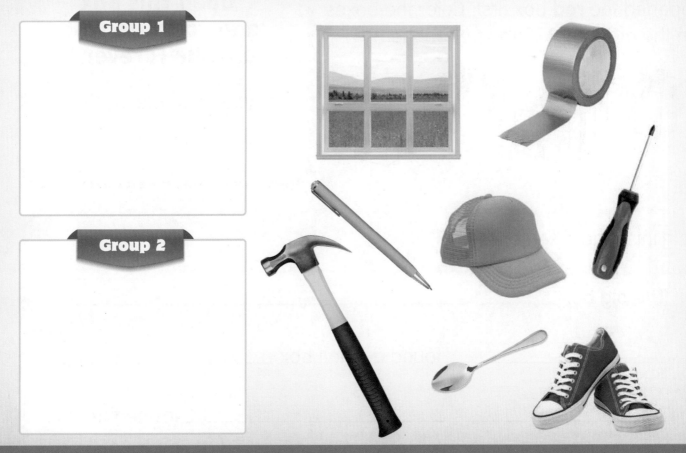

Group 1

Group 2

SKILLS: deduce, compose, decide

Determine
Boxes

What are 3 things you could use a shoebox for?

1. _____

2. _____

3. _____

Dora received 4 boxes for her birthday. She opened the **yellow** box after the **green** box but before the **blue** box. She opened the **red** box first. Color the boxes in the order that Dora opened them.

You found a mysterious box with a note on it that reads:

"Open this box and your life will change forever."

Will you open the box?

_____

Finish the 3 sentences.

The big box _____.

_____ found a small box _____.

_____ inside the box.

80 Things

Skill Sharpeners: Critical Thinking • EMC 3252 • © Evan-Moor Corp.

Forks and Spoons

What is the most important thing about forks?

_____

What is the most important thing about spoons?

_____

Finish the pattern.

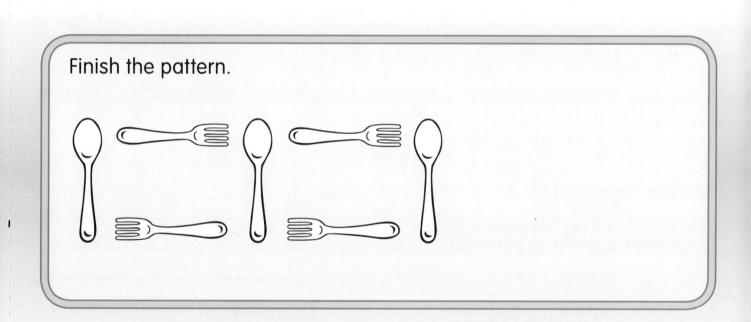

You do **not** have a spoon to eat your soup. What else could you use?

_____

You do **not** have a fork to eat your spaghetti. What else could you use?

_____

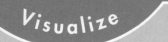

Windows and Doors

Would you see these things out your window?
Write **D** for **definitely**. Write **M** for **maybe**. Write **N** for **no**.

_____ trees   _____ dogs   _____ people

_____ cars   _____ flowers   _____ beds

_____ tigers   _____ cows   _____ squirrels

Think about the front door of your house.

What is it made of? _____

Does the door swing in or out? _____

What is the first thing you see
inside when you open your door?

_____

What is the first thing you see
outside when you open your door?

_____

Draw your
door handle.

Skill Sharpeners: Critical Thinking • EMC 3252 • © Evan-Moor Corp.

Shoes and Socks

Don't look!
What color are your socks?

_____

What color are the bottoms
of your shoes?

_____

What size shoe do you wear?

_____

What size shoe do you think you
will wear when you are grown up?

_____

How are shoes the **same** as socks?

_____

How are shoes **different** from socks?

_____

Draw the other sock.

Color them the same.

Determine

Tools

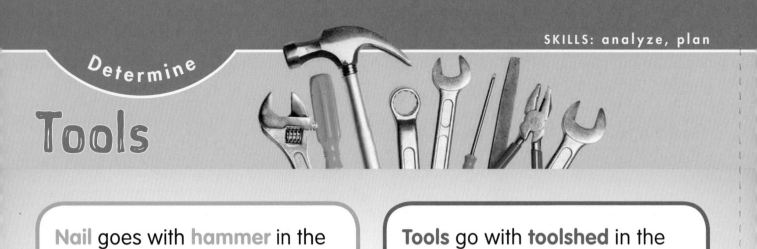

Nail goes with hammer in the same way that screw goes with

_____.

Tools go with toolshed in the same way that books go with

_____.

Draw a line to match the tool to the word that describes what it does.

pound   measure   cut   turn   grip

You are building a birdhouse. List everything you will need.

1. _____

2. _____

3. _____

4. _____

5. _____

6. _____

Hats

What are 3 reasons people wear hats?

1. _____

2. _____

3. _____

What is wrong with this picture?

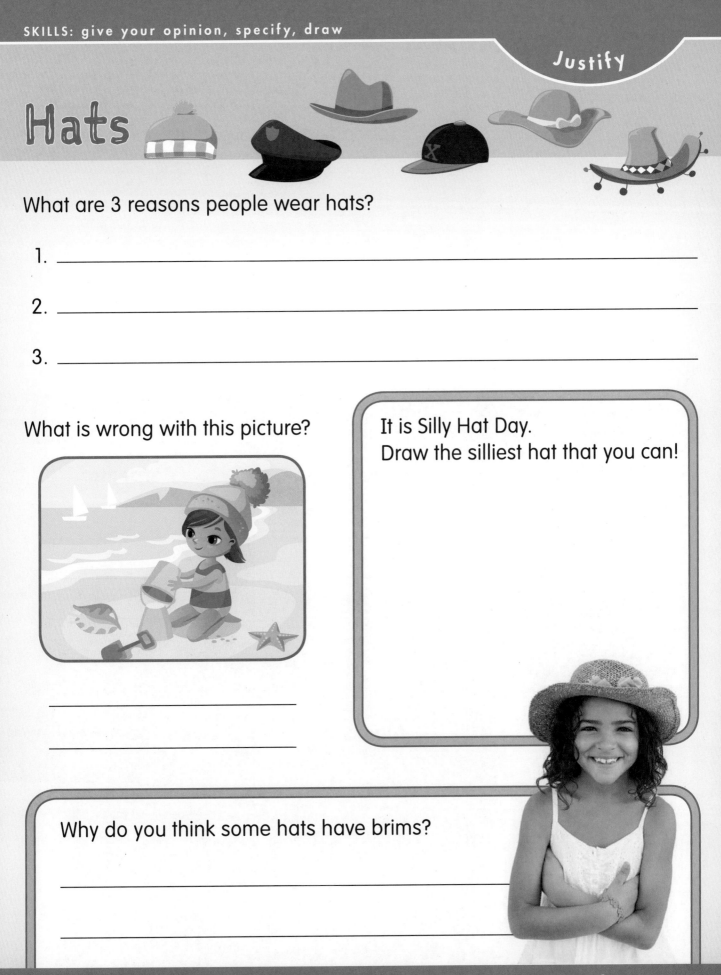

_____

_____

It is Silly Hat Day.
Draw the silliest hat that you can!

Why do you think some hats have brims?

_____

_____

Predict

Pockets

What are 3 things that each of these people might have in his or her pockets?

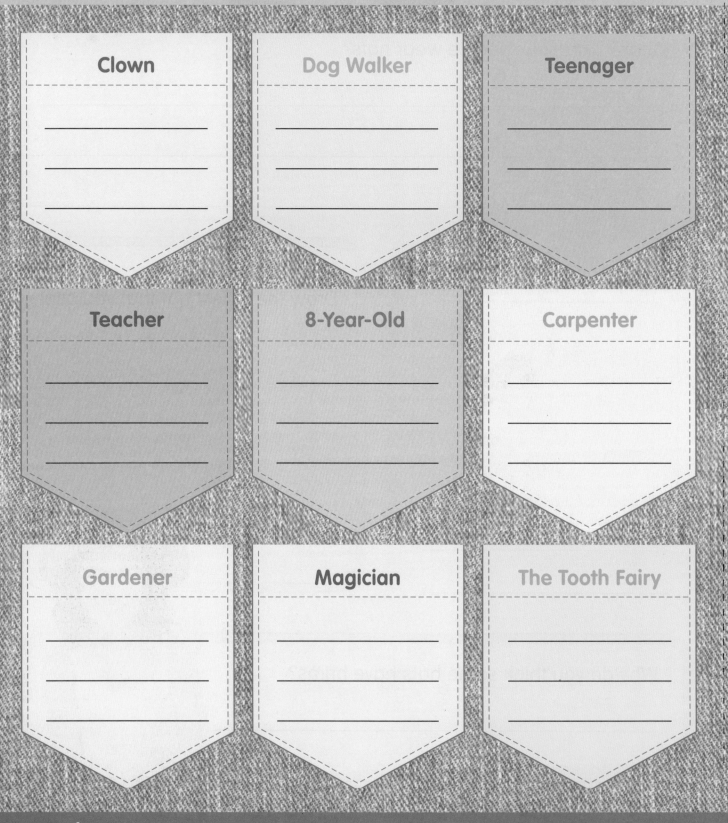

Clown

_____

_____

_____

Dog Walker

_____

_____

_____

Teenager

_____

_____

_____

Teacher

_____

_____

_____

8-Year-Old

_____

_____

_____

Carpenter

_____

_____

_____

Gardener

_____

_____

_____

Magician

_____

_____

_____

The Tooth Fairy

_____

_____

_____

Skill Sharpeners: Critical Thinking • EMC 3252 • © Evan-Moor Corp.

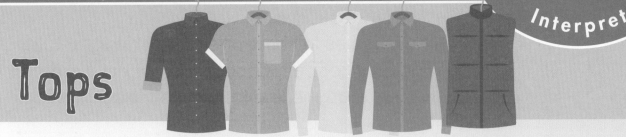

Tops

At Jamal's shirt shop, he sells only tops. Use the chart to answer the questions about what Jamal sold today.

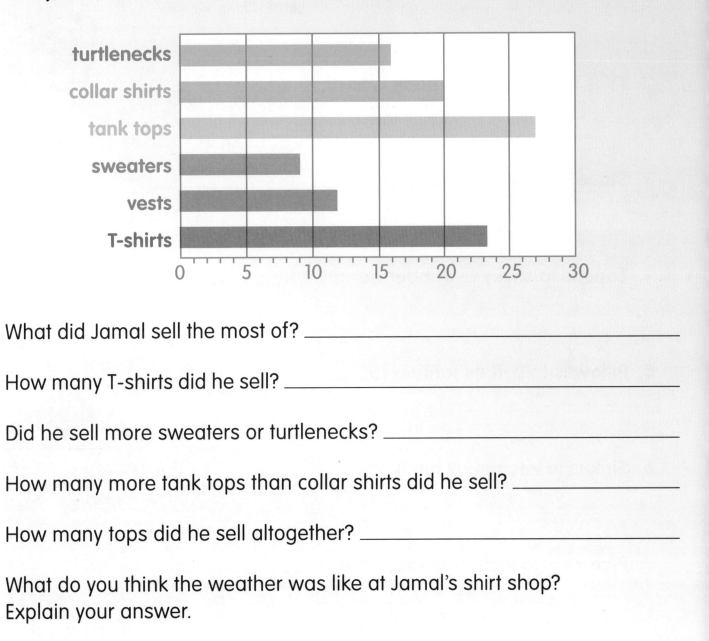

What did Jamal sell the most of? _____

How many T-shirts did he sell? _____

Did he sell more sweaters or turtlenecks? _____

How many more tank tops than collar shirts did he sell? _____

How many tops did he sell altogether? _____

What do you think the weather was like at Jamal's shirt shop? Explain your answer.

_____

_____

Compare
Analogies

Analogies tell how one pair of things relates to another pair. Choose the correct word and write it on the line to complete each analogy.

1. **Bed** is to **sleeping** as **chair** is to _____.
(table, sitting, wood)

2. **TV** is to **watching** as **book** is to _____.
(reading, words, story)

3. **Stove** is to **hot** as **freezer** is to _____.
(big, kitchen, cold)

4. **Tape** is to **sticky** as **rubber band** is to _____.
(stretchy, soft, long)

5. **Pillow** is to **soft** as **table** is to _____.
(wood, hard, dinner)

6. **Sink** is to **kitchen** as **tub** is to _____.
(water, bath, bathroom)

7. **Picture** is to **wall** as **curtain** is to _____.
(window, mirror, fabric)

8. **Sponge** is to **washing** as **broom** is to _____.
(handle, brush, sweeping)

Skill Sharpeners: Critical Thinking • EMC 3252 • © Evan-Moor Corp.

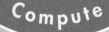

Word Problems

Clay looked at his outdoor thermometer in the morning. The temperature was 45°. In the afternoon the temperature was 62°. How much warmer was it in the afternoon than in the morning?

Work Space:

_____ degrees warmer

The weatherman reported that the high temperature for the day was 15° higher than the low temperature. If the high temperature was 81°, what was the low temperature?

Work Space:

_____ degrees

Clay has a temperature of 102°. His mother gave him some medicine. The medicine brought his temperature down to 99°. How much did his temperature drop?

Work Space:

_____ degrees

Clay's normal body temperature is 98°. Today he is not feeling well and has a temperature of 103°. How much did his temperature rise?

Work Space:

_____ degrees

Create

Paper Hat

Follow the directions to make a paper hat:

1. Cut out the pattern on page 91. Fold corner to corner.

fold

2. Fold the right corner to the middle of the other side.

fold

3. Fold the left corner to the middle of the other side.

fold

4. Fold one top piece down.

fold

5. Turn it over and fold down the other top piece.

fold

6. Color and decorate the hat. Now find someone or something small enough to wear it!

Things We Like

☑ I Did It! Check each activity as you complete it.

Be on the Lookout!

How many things on pages 95–101 do you like? Count
them and write the number here: _____

Facts About Things We Like

Read about things we like, then answer the questions on the following pages.

Have you ever thought about how many different things you like? You may like foods, toys, sports, books, music, and many other things. Our world is full of so many things to like!

Do you ever wonder why you like to eat certain foods or read certain types of books? It may not be something you think about often, but you may learn something about yourself if you give it some thought.

Why do you like to play soccer at recess instead of four-square? Maybe you enjoy being part of a team and working together.

Why do you like to draw? Maybe you like to create things with your hands.

Why do you like to read instead of watch TV? Maybe you like to use your imagination and create pictures of the story in your mind.

Sometimes the things we like just come naturally to us. For example, What's your favorite color?

What kinds of clothes do you like to wear?

What kind of weather do you like best?

Do your friends like the same things you do, or do they like different things? It's okay to like different things. What you like is part of what makes you, you!

You will grow and change, and the things you like will change, too. It's a good idea to try new things. Who knows? You might like them!

I Like These!

Tell why you like each thing.

cookies: _____

balloons: _____

music: _____

balls: _____

Put these things into 2 groups. Write the names in the boxes.
Tell someone about the groups you made.

Group 1

Group 2

Conclude

Balls

I am very heavy. I have 3 holes.
What ball am I?

_____

I am brown. I am not round.
What ball am I?

_____

I am orange. I am bouncy.
What ball am I?

_____

Which does not belong?

basketball   soccer ball   golf ball   playground ball

Why?

_____

Number the balls from 1 to 5 in order of size. The smallest ball should be 1.

_____ beach ball

_____ gum ball

_____ baseball

_____ soccer ball

_____ golf ball

Draw the other half of each ball.

Skill Sharpeners: Critical Thinking • EMC 3252 • © Evan-Moor Corp.

Describe

Cookies

How does a cookie...

taste? _____

smell? _____

look? _____

sound? _____

feel? _____

Draw 4 different cookies.
What kinds are they?

Pretend that you are making cookies. Make a ✔ next to the ingredients that you will **definitely** need. **Circle** ingredients that you **might** need. **Cross out** ingredients that you do **not** need.

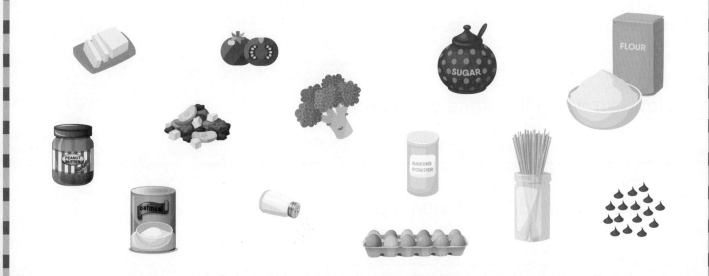

Things 97

Determine

Music

What is one of the first songs you ever learned? _____

How many songs do you think you know now? _____

What would you have if you combined a guitar and a trumpet? Draw it.

Circle the symbol that does not belong.

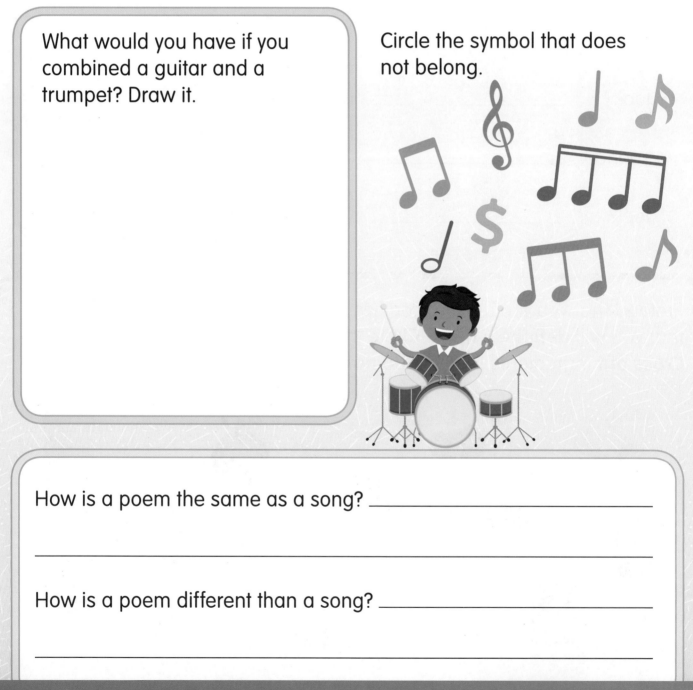

How is a poem the same as a song? _____

_____

How is a poem different than a song? _____

_____

Skill Sharpeners: Critical Thinking • EMC 3252 • © Evan-Moor Corp.

Crayons

Color these crayons with your 3 favorite colors.

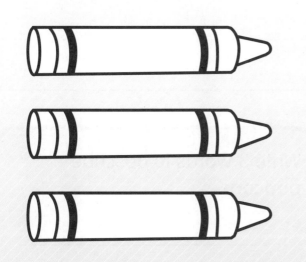

Draw a picture.
Use your 3 favorite colors.

What do you think would happen to your crayons if you…

left them in the sun? _____

dropped a book on them? _____

put them in water? _____

Finish the pattern.

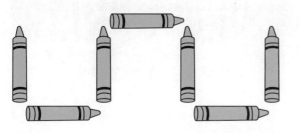

Describe
Peanuts and Popcorn

Which do you like better, peanuts or popcorn? _____

Write a sentence using the words **peanuts**, **popcorn**, and **snack**.

_____

_____

Write 3 words to describe **peanuts**.	Write 3 words to describe **popcorn**.
1. _____	1. _____
2. _____	2. _____
3. _____	3. _____

What price should each size of popcorn be?

_____   _____ $2.50   _____   _____

Crazy About Crayons

Compare

Use this graph to compare the number of crayons the children have.
Use one of these symbols in each box below.

> more than   **<** less than   **=** equal to

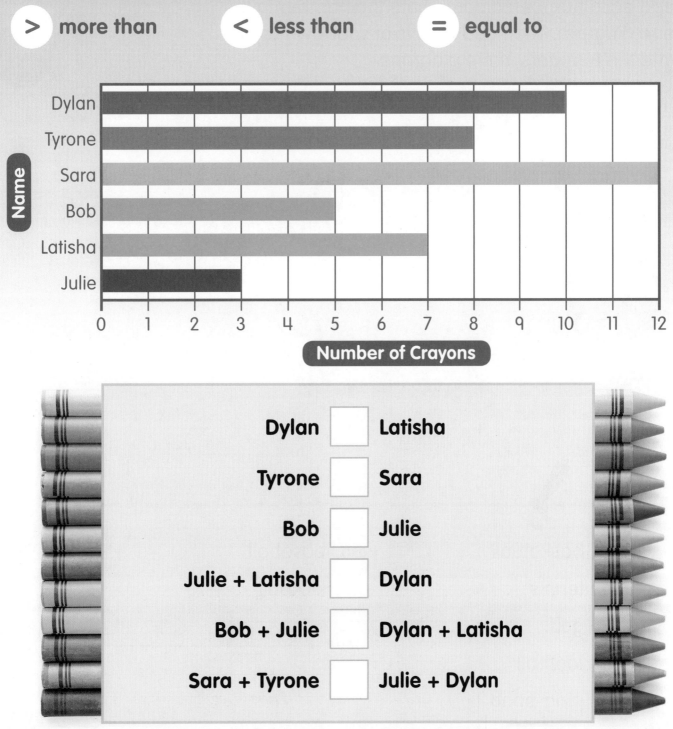

Name

| | Dylan | Tyrone | Sara | Bob | Latisha | Julie |

Number of Crayons

Dylan ☐ Latisha

Tyrone ☐ Sara

Bob ☐ Julie

Julie + Latisha ☐ Dylan

Bob + Julie ☐ Dylan + Latisha

Sara + Tyrone ☐ Julie + Dylan

Categorize

Play Ball!

Some balls are thrown. Other balls are hit or kicked. Read each numbered item. Write the number in the Venn diagram. Then add 2 balls of your own and write the numbers in the diagram.

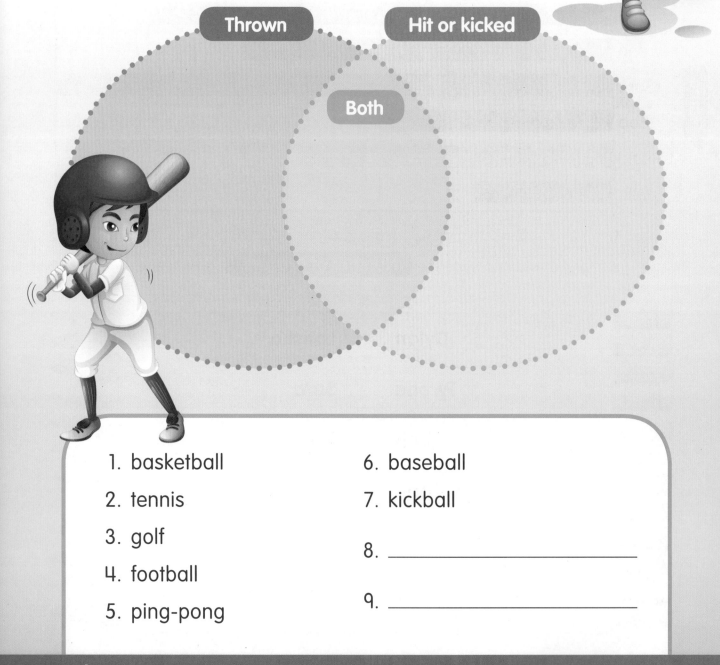

Thrown

Hit or kicked

Both

1. basketball
2. tennis
3. golf
4. football
5. ping-pong

6. baseball
7. kickball
8. _____
9. _____

Word Problems

Eli likes pickles a lot. Yesterday he ate 4 dill pickles, 2 sweet pickles, and 5 bread-and-butter pickles. Today he ate twice as many pickles.

How many pickles did Eli eat today?

Work Space:

_____ pickles

Yumi and her friends wanted popcorn. Mom made 22 cups of popcorn. The girls ate 17 cups.

How many cups of popcorn were left?

Work Space:

_____ cups of popcorn

My soccer team ate sandwiches after our practice. Each sandwich had 2 slices of bread.

How many slices of bread did it take to make 14 sandwiches?

Work Space:

_____ slices of bread

Pete had 12 peanuts. He gave $\frac{1}{3}$ of the peanuts to Bill.

How many peanuts did he give to Bill?

Work Space:

_____ peanuts

Produce

Which Color?

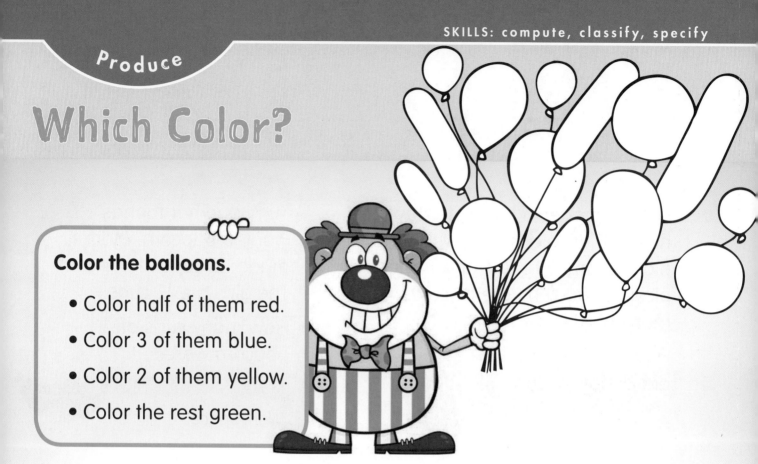

Color the balloons.

- Color half of them red.
- Color 3 of them blue.
- Color 2 of them yellow.
- Color the rest green.

Color the bar graph to show how many balloons there are of each color.

red							
blue							
yellow							
green							

Which color has the fewest balloons? _____

Which 2 colors have the same number of balloons? _____

Who's Reading?

Each of these 6 children is reading a different book. Read the clues. Then write the child's name below his or her book.

Hint: You will need to read the clues at least 2 times.

- **Meredith** and **Ramon** both chose books about dogs.

- **Christina** will need special materials in order to use her book.

- **George's** book is about mythical creatures.

- **Derek's** book is **not** about animals.

- None of the girls chose a book with the number **101** in the title.

Meredith
George
Lizzie
Ramon
Christina
Derek

_____

_____

Create

Things I Like Book

Share a book about the things you like with your family and friends!

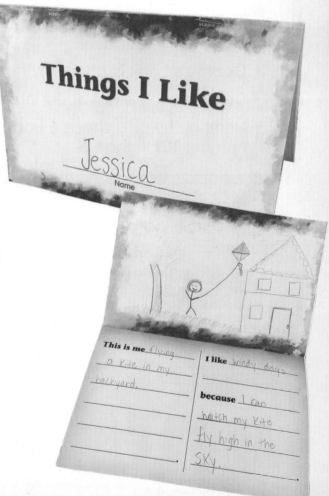

1 Follow the dashed lines to cut out pages 107 and 109.

2 Fold the pages in half.

3 Put the second folded page inside the folded cover page.

4 Complete the sentences to write the book. Then draw pictures to show what you wrote about.

5 Read your book to your family and friends.

Skill Sharpeners: Critical Thinking • EMC 3252 • © Evan-Moor Corp.

My favorite thing to do is _____

There are _____ people in my family.

I am _____ years old.

fold

staple   staple

Things I Like

_____
Name

- _____

- _____

_____

_____

because

_____

_____

I like

This is me

fold

Skill Sharpeners: Critical Thinking • EMC 3252 • © Evan-Moor Corp.

fold

This is me _____

_____

_____

_____

_____

_____ .

I like _____

_____

because _____

_____

_____

_____ .

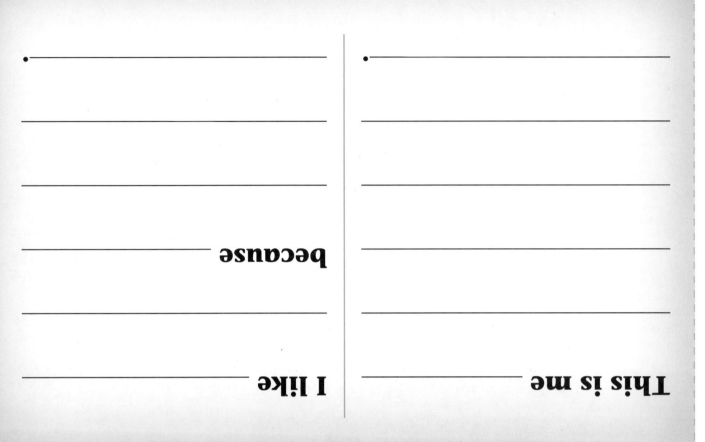

This is me

I like

because

fold

Oceans and Forests

☑ I Did It! Check each activity as you complete it.

Be on the Lookout!

How many animal names can you find on pages 113–118?
Count them and write the number here: _____

Facts About Oceans and Forests

Read about oceans and forests, then answer the questions on the following pages.

What is an ocean? An ocean is a very large body of salt water. There are five oceans on Earth. They are named the Atlantic, Arctic, Indian, Pacific, and Southern.

How many plants and animals live in the ocean? Thousands of plants and animals live in the ocean. Some live near land and some live far out in the deep ocean. These plants and animals must adapt to the place they live. They have to live in salty water. Some have learned to live where the tides move in and out. Some live deep under the water.

What is a forest? A forest is a large piece of land covered with trees and bushes. A forest is made up of many kinds of plants and animals that depend on each other for food and shelter.

Are all forests the same? There are several types of forests. Each type has its own weather and its own kind of plants and animals.

Deciduous (dee-SIJ-oo-ous) forests have trees that shed their leaves in the autumn.

Coniferous (ko-NIH-fur-us) forests have evergreen trees and shrubs that keep their leaves all year round.

Rainforests have tall, broad-leafed trees that grow close together. These trees keep their leaves. There is a thick tangle of other plants growing in and around the trees.

Tell What You Know

In the Ocean

What can you see in the ocean? Write 3 things.

1. _____ 2. _____ 3. _____

Write a sentence about the ocean. Use exactly 9 words.

_____

Words that describe **ocean** are **wet**, **blue**, **salty**, and **sandy**. What words can you use to describe the things you might find in the ocean?

_____

_____

_____

_____

You are going to swim and play in the ocean. Circle the 3 most important things to do.

stay near lifeguard   watch the waves

drink water   wear a swimsuit

stay near shore   eat lunch

bring a surfboard   tell someone

It takes 30 cups (240 grams) of sand to build a sand castle. If you can fill a bucket with 3 cups (24 grams) of sand, how many buckets do you need to build a sand castle?

_____ buckets

Tell What You Know

In the Forest

What can you see in the forest? Write 3 things.

1. _____   2. _____   3. _____

Write a sentence about the forest. Use exactly 7 words.

_____

Forest is another word for **woods**. What are other words for these things you might find in the woods?

rabbit _____

trail _____

creek _____

stone _____

twig _____

burrow _____

You are going for a hike in the forest. Circle the 3 most important things to bring.

compass	book	binoculars
whistle	map	first-aid kit
water	hat	flashlight
bug spray	snack	

If you walk 3 miles in an hour, how far will you walk in 90 minutes?

_____ miles

Skill Sharpeners: Critical Thinking • EMC 3252 • © Evan-Moor Corp.

Compare

Oceans and Forests

Read each numbered item. Write the number in the Venn diagram.
Then make up 2 of your own and write the numbers in the diagram.

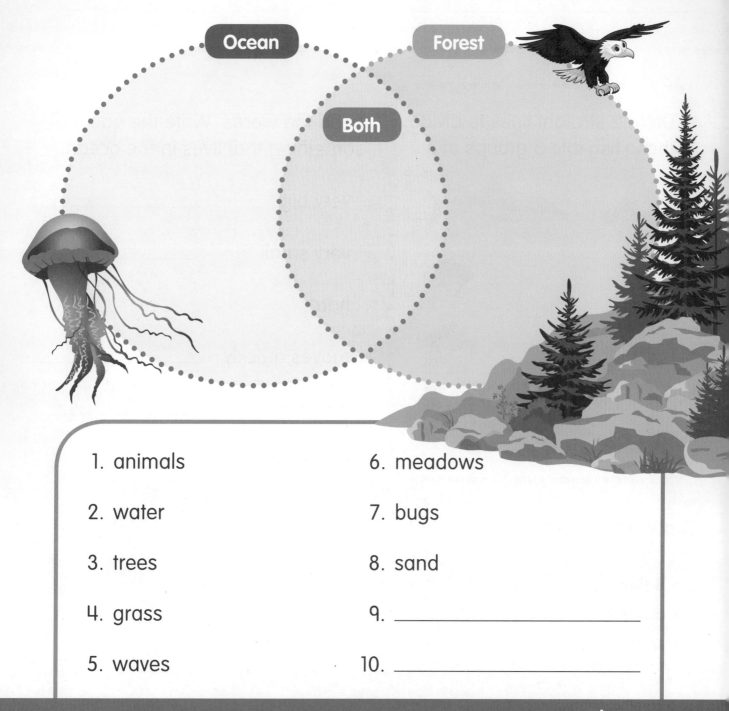

Ocean

Forest

Both

1. animals

2. water

3. trees

4. grass

5. waves

6. meadows

7. bugs

8. sand

9. _____

10. _____

Under the Sea

Fish goes with **scales** in the same way that **bear** goes with

_____.

Fish goes with **fins** in the same way that **bird** goes with

_____.

Draw 2 straight lines to divide these fish into 3 groups of 3.

Read the words. Write the name of something that lives in the ocean.

very big _____

very small _____

hard _____

moves quickly _____

has arms _____

people eat it _____

Draw Freddy Fish.
He has:

- **3 fins**
- **a big tail**
- **spots**

Skill Sharpeners: Critical Thinking • EMC 3252 • © Evan-Moor Corp.

Categorize

Forest Finds

Add 2 more to each list.

raccoon, deer, rabbit, _____, _____

beetle, mosquito, butterfly, _____, _____

Name something in the woods that is…

soft _____

hard _____

rough _____

sharp _____

Draw lines to match the animals with their descriptions. Be careful: You may match only 1 description to each animal.

woodpecker	**brown**
squirrel	**bushy tail**
deer	**long ears**
skunk	**black and white**
rabbit	**can fly**

What does this say?

A
WOwalkODS

_____

_____

Determine

Waves of 8

Color each box that contains a multiple of 8 to find the name of a fascinating ocean creature.

8 O	9 A	12 T	25 M	30 L
15 S	20 H	36 E	16 C	21 L
27 N	24 T	45 O	42 R	50 S
32 O	54 E	22 D	40 P	10 B
48 U	17 W	49 A	18 G	56 S

Draw a picture of this ocean creature. It should have _____ arms.

Solve

Through the Trees

We are going for a walk through the woods. As we walk along, we will see lots of things that begin with **tr-** and **thr-**. Use words from the word box to fill in the crossword puzzle.

Word Box

true	thread	tractor	try
three	triangle	throat	track

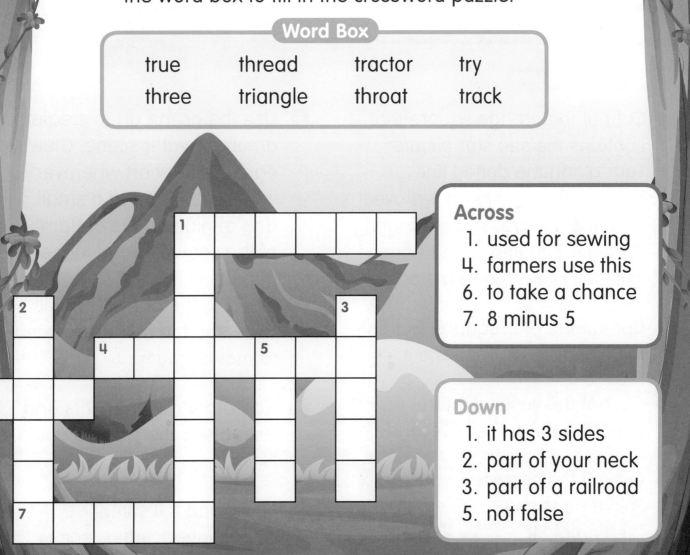

Across
1. used for sewing
4. farmers use this
6. to take a chance
7. 8 minus 5

Down
1. it has 3 sides
2. part of your neck
3. part of a railroad
5. not false

Create

An Ocean Scene

Imagine you are under the ocean. Create a scene that shows what you see!

What You Need:

- seaweed, sea star, and shells from page 121
- a large piece of blue paper
- glue   • scissors

Optional: markers, glitter, sand, and anything else you'd like to use to decorate the picture or make more sea animals.

What You Do:

1. Cut out the orange square that contains the sea star picture. Tear along the dotted line around the sea star to remove it from the square. You are tearing instead of cutting so the edges will look like a real sea star.

2. Cut out the pink square. Cut out the conch shell. Decorate it.

3. Cut out the yellow square. Cut out the scallop shell. Decorate it.

4. Cut out the seaweed. Fold it as shown, then unfold it.

5. Use the ocean art to create an underwater scene. Glue each piece of art wherever you'd like. **Tip** Put a small dab of glue on the bottom of the seaweed and in the middle so it is not completely glued to the page. This will allow the top of the seaweed to move around.

6. Add other ocean plants and animals to the scene if you'd like to.

7. Show and tell someone about your ocean scene.

Skill Sharpeners: Critical Thinking • EMC 3252 • © Evan-Moor Corp.

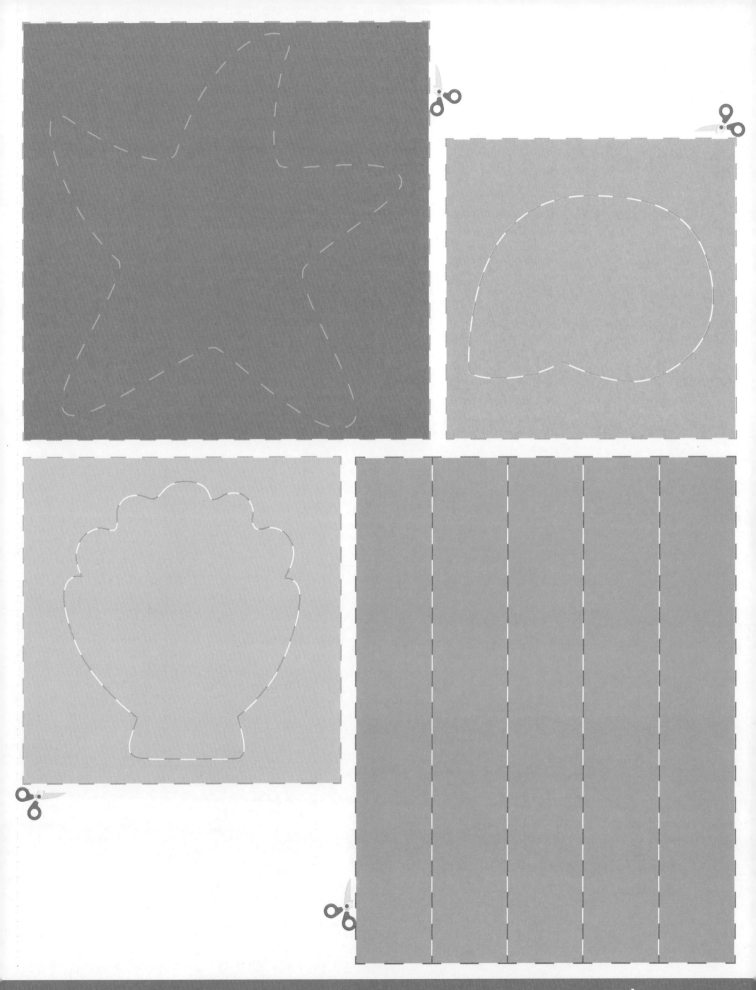

Deserts

✔ I Did It! Check each activity as you complete it.

Be on the Lookout!

How many cactus plants can you find on pages 125–132?

Count them and write the number here: _____

Facts About Deserts

Read about deserts, then answer the
questions on the following pages.

What is a desert?

A desert is a very dry place. A desert gets very
little rainfall. A lot of the rain goes back into the
air quickly because of the heat. A desert seems
empty because few plants grow there. The
plants and animals in a desert habitat must
be able to live without much water. They
must be able to stand a lot of heat during
the day. Because there are no clouds to trap
the heat, the desert can be very cold at night.

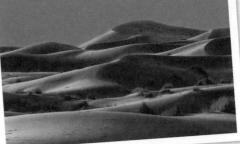

Are all deserts the same?

There are different kinds of deserts. Some deserts are
covered in sand. The wind blows the sand into mounds or
hills called **dunes**. Some deserts are covered with rocky cliffs
and hills. Blowing winds carve rocks into strange shapes.
Other deserts are flat, dry plains of soil and gravel. There
are even deserts that are not hot. Deserts at high altitudes
are cold, but are still places with very little rainfall.

What animals live in a desert?

Many different animals live in deserts around the world. They can survive
with very little water. Some desert animals get water from the plants or seeds
they eat. Some predators get water from the animals they eat. Some animals
get the water they need by licking the water that collects on plants and rocks
during the night. Heat is a problem, too. Some animals rest in shady spots.
Some live underground and only come out at night. Some are covered with
hard scales that keep them from drying out in the hot sun.

Skill Sharpeners: Critical Thinking • EMC 3252 • © Evan-Moor Corp.

Tell What You Know

In the Desert

What can you see in the desert?
Write 3 things.

1. _____ 2. _____ 3. _____

Write a sentence about the desert. Use exactly 6 words.

_____

Words that describe **desert** are **hot**, **dry**, and **sandy**. What words can you use to describe the things you might find in the desert?

cactus _____

sand _____

owl _____

lizard _____

tortoise _____

fox _____

You are going on a hike in the desert. Circle the 3 most important things to bring.

compass   water

sunglasses   swimsuit

hat   food

heavy coat   camera

If you see 4 desert animals every 30 minutes, how many animals will you have seen in 3 hours?

_____ animals

Produce

Red Hot

Choose the correct word to complete the sentence.

| habitats   hot   wet   wild |

The desert, the rainforest, and the grasslands are all _____.

How many words can you write that rhyme with **hot**?

_____

_____

Circle the word that is an antonym for **hot**.

cold   heat   sunny   warm

Circle the word that does **not** belong.

lizard   duck   roadrunner   snake

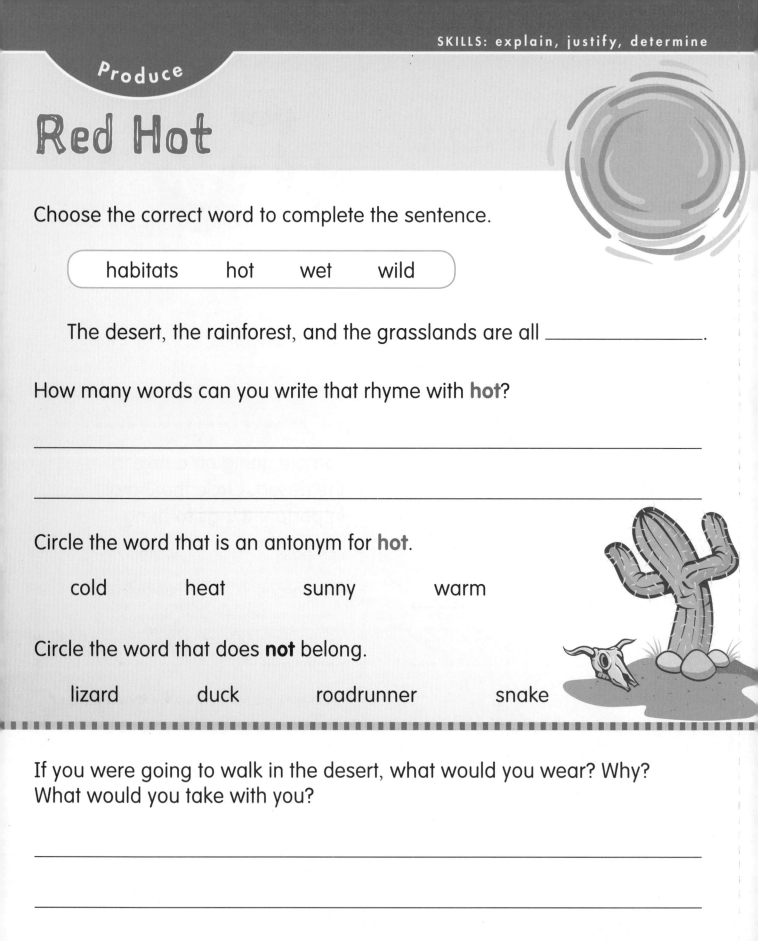

If you were going to walk in the desert, what would you wear? Why?
What would you take with you?

_____

_____

_____

Skill Sharpeners: Critical Thinking • EMC 3252 • © Evan-Moor Corp.

Roadrunner

Draw

Follow the directions to draw a roadrunner. Then color your roadrunner and answer the questions.

Where does your roadrunner live? _____

What does it eat? _____

What does it like to do? _____

Construct

Think Fast!

Use the letters in **DESERT ROADRUNNER** to make lots of words. Write them on the lines below.

red

toad

sun

Word Problems

Jakob went for a walk with Grandpa. They left home at 11 o'clock. "Be back in 4 hours," said Jakob's mother.

At what time did they have to be back?

Show your answer on the clock.

_____ o'clock

Jakob likes to go on walks with Grandpa. Last month they walked on 9 days. This month they walked on 8 days.

On how many days did they walk in the last 2 months? _____ days

How many days do you think they will walk next month? _____ days

Tell why.

_____

_____

Change

From Lizard to Turtle

Turn a lizard into a turtle in just 6 steps. Read each clue and rewrite the word. Change only 1 letter on each line until you have a turtle!

A B C D E F G H I J K L M N O P Q R S T U V W X Y Z

L I Z A R D

Change the 4th letter in the alphabet to the 5th.	L	I	Z	A	R	E
Change the 3rd letter to an R.						
Change the letter with just 2 straight lines to a T.						
Make the 4th letter the same as the 1st letter.						
Change the 5th letter to an L.						
Change I into the last vowel in the alphabet.						

What Doesn't Belong?

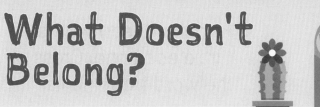

Categorize

Cross out the word in each row that does **not** belong.
Circle the word in each row that tells about all the other words.

1. cactus   tree   plants   flower   water

2. dry   sandy   hot   wet   desert

3. walking   moving   singing   jumping   running

4. snake   fox   owl   animals   habitat

5. wind   weather   sun   umbrella   rain

Now write 2 rows of your own words. Then, in each row, ask someone to cross out the word that does not belong and circle the word that tells about all the other words.

_____   _____   _____   _____   _____

_____   _____   _____   _____   _____

Find

Desert Words

Find the desert words. Circle each one. Cross off the word from the list.

Word Box

CACTUS	LIZARD
DESERT	HABITAT
OWL	DRY
FOX	HOT

B	X	N	M	L	K	F	O	X
Z	P	I	H	Q	J	I	R	L
W	O	T	A	C	H	G	D	I
G	O	A	H	A	C	F	E	Z
E	W	C	A	C	T	U	S	A
S	L	A	B	E	S	R	E	R
M	K	B	I	Z	A	D	R	D
T	R	F	T	D	R	Y	T	V
Z	S	G	A	P	S	E	L	O
Q	X	R	T	H	O	T	Y	X

Determine

Flying High

This graph tells about the colors of kites children were flying in the desert. **Each kite picture stands for 2 kites.** Use the graph to help you answer the questions.

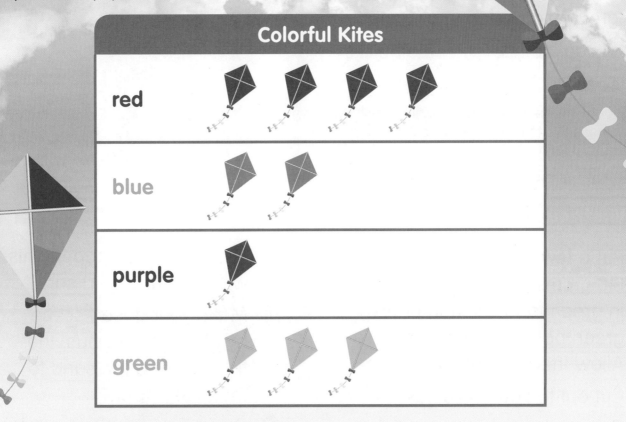

Colorful Kites

red	🪁 🪁 🪁 🪁
blue	🪁 🪁
purple	🪁
green	🪁 🪁 🪁

1. How many children have kites? _____ children

2. How many more children have red kites than purple kites? _____ children

3. Which color do most children have? _____

4. How many children have blue kites? _____ children

Places 133

Create

Feel the Cactus

Create a cactus that looks and feels prickly!

What You Need:

- cactus, red paper, and tan paper from page 135
- a piece of blue paper
- green food coloring or paint
- uncooked rice
- toothpicks
- scissors
- glue

Optional: markers, glitter, sand, and anything else you'd like to use to decorate the picture or make it fun to feel.

What You Do:

1. Put a few toothpicks and $\frac{1}{3}$ cup (40 grams) uncooked rice granules in green food coloring or use green paint to paint them. Allow them to dry.

2. Cut out the green cactus.

3. Cut out the red squares. Fold each square in half two times. Cut a wavy pattern around the edges of the squares to make a flower. Unfold the squares. Pinch the middle of the flower on the bottom as shown to make a cactus flower.

4. Cut out the tan paper. This will be your desert sand.

5. Make your desert scene by gluing the cactus, the flowers, and the sand to the blue paper.

6. Glue the rice to the cactus. Glue toothpicks to the cactus. Add desert animals to the scene if you'd like to.

7. After your cactus dries, ask someone to touch it. Tell them about your desert scene.

Skill Sharpeners: Critical Thinking • EMC 3252 • © Evan-Moor Corp.

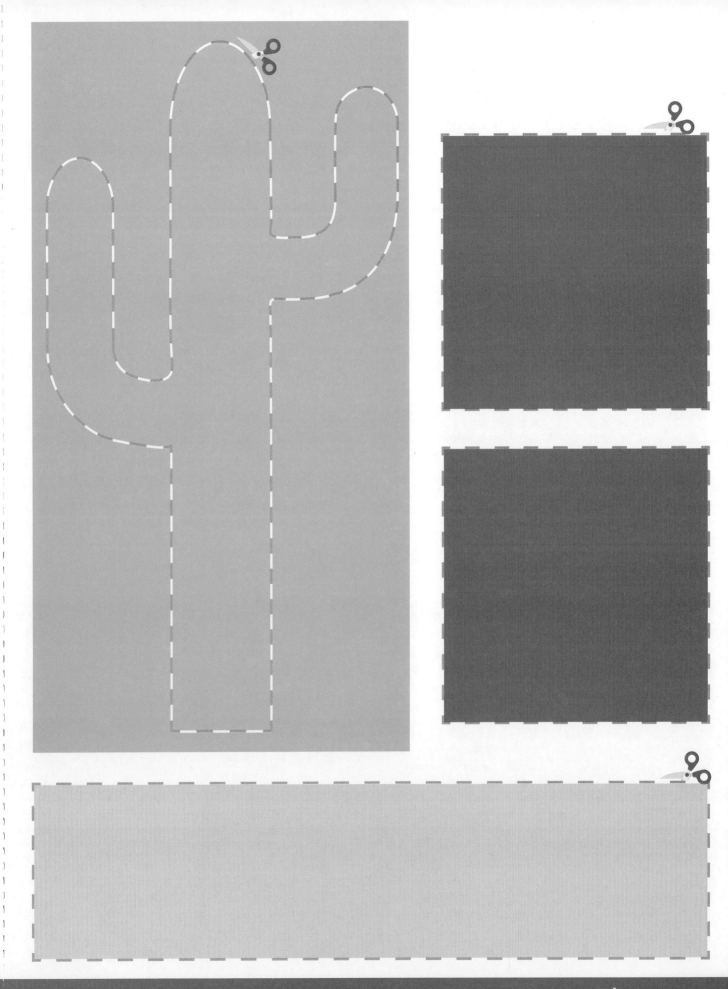

Answer Key

Page 9

Alligators

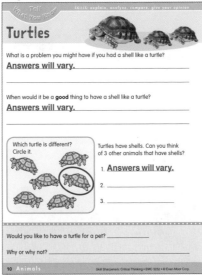

Write 2 sentences about alligators.

1. An alligator **Answers will vary.**

2. _____ alligator.

Write F if the statement is a fact. Write O if it is an opinion.

F Alligators have sharp teeth.

F Alligators are reptiles.

O Alligators are too big.

F Alligators can swim.

Can you think of 4 other animals with sharp teeth?

1. **Answers will vary.**
2. _____
3. _____
4. _____

Draw an alligator with a bunny tail and bunny ears.

Drawings will vary.

Page 10

Turtles

What is a problem you might have if you had a shell like a turtle?

Answers will vary.

When would it be a **good** thing to have a shell like a turtle?

Answers will vary.

Which turtle is different? Circle it.

Turtles have shells. Can you think of 3 other animals that have shells?

1. **Answers will vary.**
2. _____
3. _____

Would you like to have a turtle for a pet? _____

Why or why not? _____

Page 11

Alligators and Turtles

Read each numbered item. Does it tell about alligators, turtles, or both? Write the number in the Venn diagram. Then make up 2 of your own and write the numbers in the diagram.

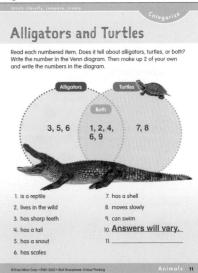

Alligators: **3, 5, 6** Both: **1, 2, 4, 6, 9** Turtles: **7, 8**

1. is a reptile
2. lives in the wild
3. has sharp teeth
4. has a tail
5. has a snout
6. has scales
7. has a shell
8. moves slowly
9. can swim
10. **Answers will vary.**
11. _____

Page 12

Word Problems

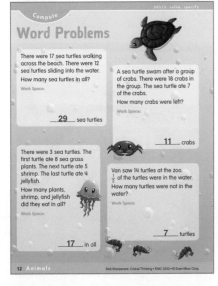

There were 17 sea turtles walking across the beach. There were 12 sea turtles sliding into the water. How many sea turtles in all?

Work Space:

29 sea turtles

A sea turtle swam after a group of crabs. There were 18 crabs in the group. The sea turtle ate 7 of the crabs. How many crabs were left?

Work Space:

11 crabs

There were 3 sea turtles. The first turtle ate 8 sea grass plants. The next turtle ate 5 shrimp. The last turtle ate 4 jellyfish. How many plants, shrimp, and jellyfish did they eat in all?

Work Space:

17 in all

Van saw 14 turtles at the zoo. $\frac{1}{2}$ of the turtles were in the water. How many turtles were not in the water?

Work Space:

7 turtles

Page 13

Snack Time!

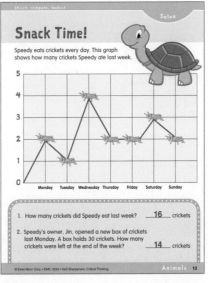

Speedy eats crickets every day. This graph shows how many crickets Speedy ate last week.

1. How many crickets did Speedy eat last week? **16** crickets

2. Speedy's owner, Jin, opened a new box of crickets last Monday. A box holds 30 crickets. How many crickets were left at the end of the week? **14** crickets

Page 14

Join the Group

Change the colored letter in each word to make a new word that fits in the group. Write the new word on the line.

Group: Pets
- cap → **cat**
- log → **dog**
- dish → **fish**

Group: Fruits
- bear → **pear**
- plus → **plum**
- gripe → **grape**

Group: Things with Wheels
- can → **cab**
- bake → **bike**
- track → **truck**

Group: Birds
- own → **owl**
- deck → **duck**
- hack → **hawk**

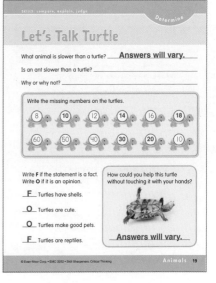

Page 17

It's Gator Time!

What do alligators eat?
fish, birds, deer

Write 3 words that describe alligators.

1. **Answers will vary.**
2. _____
3. _____

An alligator has about 80 teeth. How many teeth do 2 alligators have?

160 teeth

If an alligator lost 6 teeth, how many would it have left?

74 teeth left

Which alligator is different? Circle it.

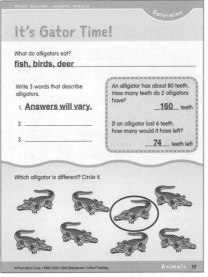

Page 18

Gator Words

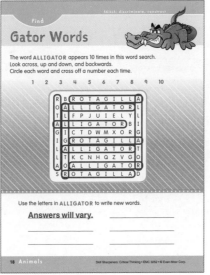

The word **ALLIGATOR** appears 10 times in this word search. Look across, up and down, and backwards. Circle each word and cross off a number each time.

1 2 3 4 5 6 7 8 9 10

R	B	R	O	T	A	G	I	L	L	A
O	A	L	L	I	G	A	T	O	R	L
T	L	F	P	J	U	I	E	L	Y	L
A	L	L	I	G	A	T	O	R	B	I
G	I	C	T	D	W	M	X	O	R	G
I	G	A	L	L	I	G	A	T	O	R
L	A	L	L	I	G	A	T	O	R	T
L	T	K	C	N	H	Q	Z	V	G	O
A	O	A	L	L	I	G	A	T	O	R
S	R	O	T	A	G	I	L	L	A	D

Use the letters in **ALLIGATOR** to write new words.

Answers will vary.

Page 19

Let's Talk Turtle

What animal is slower than a turtle? **Answers will vary.**

Is an ant slower than a turtle? _____

Why or why not? _____

Write the missing numbers on the turtles.

8 10 12 14 16 18

60 50 40 30 20 10

Write F if the statement is a fact. Write O if it is an opinion.

F Turtles have shells.

O Turtles are cute.

O Turtles make good pets.

F Turtles are reptiles.

How could you help this turtle without touching it with your hands?

Answers will vary.

Page 29

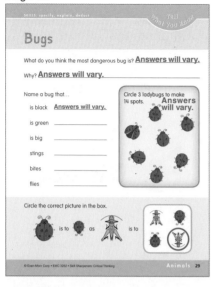

Bugs

What do you think the most dangerous bug is? **Answers will vary.**

Why? **Answers will vary.**

Name a bug that...

is black **Answers will vary.**

is green _____

is big _____

stings _____

bites _____

flies _____

Circle 3 ladybugs to make 14 spots. **Answers will vary.**

Circle the correct picture in the box.

Page 30

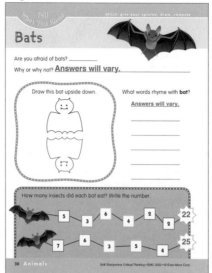

Bats

Are you afraid of bats? _____

Why or why not? **Answers will vary.**

Draw this bat upside down.

What words rhyme with **bat**?

Answers will vary.

How many insects did each bat eat? Write the number.

5 3 6 4 2 → **22**

7 2 6 3 5 4 → **25**

Page 31

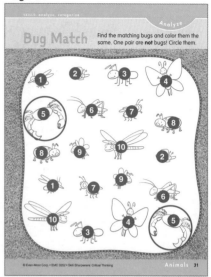

Bug Match Find the matching bugs and color them the same. One pair are **not** bugs! Circle them.

Page 32

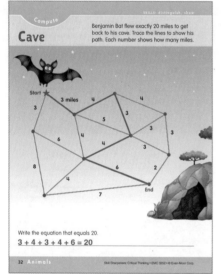

Cave

Benjamin Bat flew exactly 20 miles to get back to his cave. Trace the lines to show his path. Each number shows how many miles.

Write the equation that equals 20.

3 + 4 + 3 + 4 + 6 = 20

Page 33

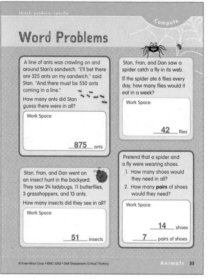

Word Problems

A line of ants was crawling on and around Stan's sandwich. "I'll bet there are 325 ants on my sandwich," said Stan. "And there must be 550 ants coming in a line."
How many ants did Stan guess there were in all?

Work Space:

875 ants

Stan, Fran, and Dan saw a spider catch a fly in its web. If the spider ate 6 flies every day, how many flies would it eat in a week?

Work Space:

42 flies

Stan, Fran, and Dan went on an insect hunt in the backyard. They saw 24 ladybugs, 11 butterflies, 3 grasshoppers, and 13 ants.
How many insects did they see in all?

51 insects

Pretend that a spider and a fly were wearing shoes.
1. How many shoes would they need in all?
2. How many **pairs** of shoes would they need?

Work Space:

14 shoes

7 pairs of shoes

Page 34

Hidden Animals

Caves are home to many animals. Unscramble the animal names below. Then find the animals in the cave and color them.

orgf **frog**   tab **bat**   tra **rat**

hifs **fish**   prised **spider**   tickerc **cricket**

Page 35

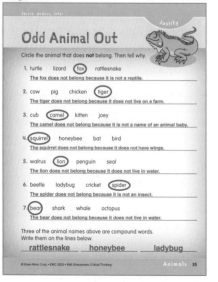

Odd Animal Out

Circle the animal that does not belong. Then tell why.

1. turtle lizard (fox) rattlesnake
   The fox does not belong because it is not a reptile.

2. cow pig chicken (tiger)
   The tiger does not belong because it does not live on a farm.

3. cub (camel) kitten joey
   The camel does not belong because it is not a name of an animal baby.

4. (squirrel) honeybee bat bird
   The squirrel does not belong because it does not have wings.

5. walrus (lion) penguin seal
   The lion does not belong because it does not live in water.

6. beetle ladybug cricket (spider)
   The spider does not belong because it is not an insect.

7. (bear) shark whale octopus
   The bear does not belong because it does not live in water.

Three of the animal names above are compound words. Write them on the lines below.

rattlesnake   **honeybee**   **ladybug**

Page 36

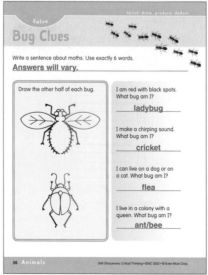

Bug Clues

Write a sentence about moths. Use exactly 6 words.
Answers will vary.

Draw the other half of each bug.

I am red with black spots. What bug am I?
ladybug

I make a chirping sound. What bug am I?
cricket

I can live on a dog or on a cat. What bug am I?
flea

I live in a colony with a queen. What bug am I?
ant/bee

Page 37

Cave Maze   Find your way through the cave maze.

Who Am I?
Solve • SKILLS: graph, conclude

Use the code to name each bat.

I am the largest bat. I have a wingspan of 6 feet (1.8 m). Who am I?

F L Y I N G
1d 2b 4b 2a 2d 1e

F O X
1d 2e 4a

I am the smallest bat. I weigh less than a penny. Who am I?

B U M B L E B E E
1b 3d 2c 1b 2b 1c 1b 1c

B A T
1b 1a 3c

I am the bat that eats blood. Who am I?

V A M P I R E
3e 1c 2c 3a 2a 3b 1c

B A T
1b 1a 3c

	a	b	c	d	e
1	A	B	E	F	G
2	I	L	M	N	O
3	P	R	T	U	V
4	X	Y			

38 Animals

Bat Connections
SKILLS: decide, change, compute • Conclude

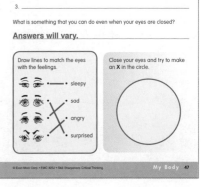

The animals on each line go together. Write why.

bat, crow, panther **are black**

bat, sparrow, bee **can fly**

bat, anteater, frog **eat insects**

bat, owl, sloth **live in trees**

Change the underlined letter to make a different word. Write the word.

B A T **Answers will vary.**

B A T _____

B A T _____

Bats eat a lot of insects—about 600 in 1 hour! About how many insects would a bat eat…

in 2 hours? **1,200** insects

in 3 hours? **1,800** insects

Write **F** if the statement is a fact. Write **O** if it is an opinion.

F Some bats are brown. **F** Bats eat insects.

O Bats are scary. **O** Bats are cute.

Animals 39

My Eyes
SKILLS: specify, infer • Tell What You Know

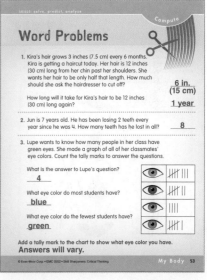

What are 3 things that you **cannot** do with your eyes closed?

1. **Answers will vary.** _____

2. _____

3. _____

What is something that you can do even when your eyes are closed?

Answers will vary. _____

Draw lines to match the eyes with the feelings.

- sleepy
- sad
- angry
- surprised

Close your eyes and try to make an **X** in the circle.

My Body 47

My Teeth
Tell What You Know • SKILLS: explain, draw, predict

How many teeth do you have? _____

How did you count them? **Answers will vary.**

How many teeth are missing? _____

Draw your smile.
Drawings will vary.

What are 3 foods that would be **easy** to eat if you did not have any teeth?
1. _____
2. _____
3. _____

What are 3 foods that would be **hard** to eat if you did not have any teeth?
1. _____
2. _____
3. _____

48 My Body

A Hairy Riddle
Solve • SKILLS: deduct, explain

Use the code to find the answer to the riddle.

1	2	3	4	5	6	7	8	9	10	11	12	13
A	B	C	D	E	F	G	H	I	J	K	L	M
14	15	16	17	18	19	20	21	22	23	24	25	26
N	O	P	Q	R	S	T	U	V	W	X	Y	Z

Why do barbers make good drivers?

| 2 | 5 | 3 | 1 | 21 | 19 | 5 | | 20 | 8 | 5 | 25 |
| B | E | C | A | U | S | E | | T | H | E | Y |

| 11 | 14 | 15 | 23 | | 1 | 12 | 12 | | 20 | 8 | 5 |
| K | N | O | W | | A | L | L | | T | H | E |

| 19 | 8 | 15 | 18 | 20 | 3 | 21 | 20 | 19 |
| S | H | O | R | T | C | U | T | S |

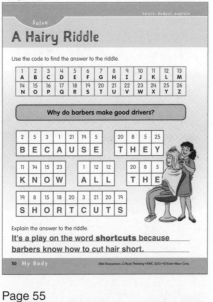

Explain the answer to the riddle.
It's a play on the word shortcuts because barbers know how to cut hair short.

50 My Body

Word Problems
SKILLS: solve, predict, analyze • Compute

1. Kira's hair grows 3 inches (7.5 cm) every 6 months. Kira is getting a haircut today. Her hair is 12 inches (30 cm) long from her chin past her shoulders. She wants her hair to be only half that length. How much should she ask the hairdresser to cut off?
6 in. (15 cm)

How long will it take for Kira's hair to be 12 inches (30 cm) long again?
1 year

2. Jun is 7 years old. He has been losing 2 teeth every year since he was 4. How many teeth has he lost in all?
8

3. Lupe wants to know how many people in her class have green eyes. She made a graph of all of her classmates' eye colors. Count the tally marks to answer the questions.

What is the answer to Lupe's question?
4

What eye color do most students have?
blue

What eye color do the fewest students have?
green

Add a tally mark to the chart to show what eye color you have.
Answers will vary.

My Body 53

Open Wide!
Decide • SKILLS: justify, classify

1. Circle the one that **cannot** be a **dentist**.
a doctor   a man   (a vet)   a woman

2. Circle the word that rhymes with **tooth**.
boo   (booth)   both   broth

3. Circle the word that does **not** belong.
(cast)   cavity   tooth   pain

4. Circle the word that is a synonym for **ache**.
ask   ear   ouch   (pain)

5. In Box 1, draw foods that are not good for your teeth. In Box 2, draw foods that are good for your teeth. Add labels that name each food.

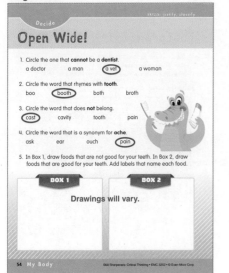

BOX 1 **BOX 2**
Drawings will vary.

54 My Body

What Is It?
SKILLS: draw conclusions, infer • Solve

Read the clue. Look at the pictures. Write the letter of the clue below the picture it tells about. Then write the word to solve the clue.

A. You hold it in your hand and use a downward motion to help you look tidy.

B. You hold it in your hand and use it with a cream to clean.

C. You use these to find out what is going on around you.

D. You have a lot of these, and they are always growing.

E. It is a thin string used to clean.

F. It washes the dirt out of your hair.

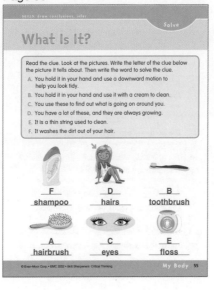

F shampoo   **D** hairs   **B** toothbrush

A hairbrush   **C** eyes   **E** floss

My Body 55

The Answer Is...
Deduce • SKILLS: determine, infer

Write the word for each clue. Then write the letters from the colored boxes to answer the riddle below.

What you put on your toothbrush
t o o t h p a s t e

A sweet food that is bad for your teeth
c a n d y

What you use to clean between your teeth
f l o s s

The pink area around your teeth
g u m s

What you use to clean your teeth
t o o t h b r u s h

What has teeth but does **not** have a mouth?
a   c o m b

56 My Body

Page 58

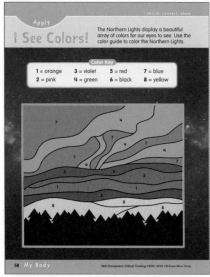

Apply

I See Colors!

The Northern Lights display a beautiful array of colors for our eyes to see. Use the color guide to color the Northern Lights.

Color Key

1 = orange	3 = violet	5 = red	7 = blue
2 = pink	4 = green	6 = black	8 = yellow

Page 63

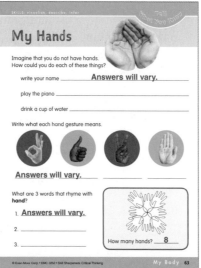

My Hands

Imagine that you do not have hands. How could you do each of these things?

write your name __ **Answers will vary.**

play the piano _____

drink a cup of water _____

Write what each hand gesture means.

Answers will vary.

What are 3 words that rhyme with **hand**?

1. **Answers will vary.**

2. _____

3. _____

How many hands? **8**

Page 64

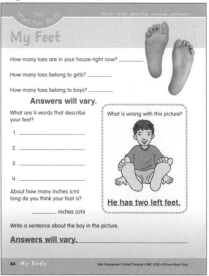

My Feet

How many toes are in your house right now? _____

How many toes belong to girls? _____

How many toes belong to boys? _____

Answers will vary.

What are 4 words that describe your feet?

1. _____

2. _____

3. _____

4. _____

About how many inches (cm) long do you think your foot is?

_____ inches (cm)

Write a sentence about the boy in the picture.

Answers will vary.

What is wrong with this picture?

He has two left feet.

Page 66

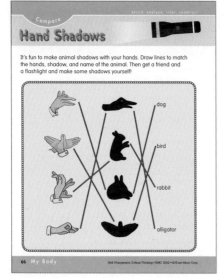

Compare

Hand Shadows

It's fun to make animal shadows with your hands. Draw lines to match the hands, shadow, and name of the animal. Then get a friend and a flashlight and make some shadows yourself!

dog

bird

rabbit

alligator

Page 67

Foot Notes

Deduce

Foot goes with **sock** in the same way that **hand** goes with **glove**

Foot goes with **toes** in the same way that **hand** goes with **fingers**

Unscramble these parts of a foot.

ELEH __ **heel**

OET __ **toe**

LOES __ **sole**

OETLINA __ **toenail**

What do you wear on your feet when...

it is hot? **Answers will vary.**

it is rainy? _____

it is nighttime? _____

they are cold? _____

What is something that you might put on your feet besides shoes or socks?

Answers will vary.

Page 68

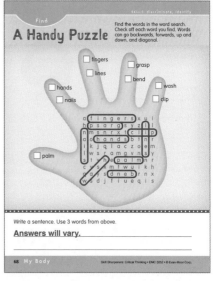

Find

A Handy Puzzle

Find the words in the word search. Check off each word you find. Words can go backwards, forwards, up and down, and diagonal.

☐ fingers ☐ grasp
☐ lines ☐ bend
☐ hands ☐ wash
☐ nails ☐ clip
☐ palm

```
a f i n g e r s x u i
h p s a r g s y z f
m s n r x c i p
o h a n d s b t n
i k j q l a c z o e m
l s r a m g v n s y
s t h e p a l m n
c s m t w u i k h
a q s d n e b r n x
w d j f i u e q i s
```

Write a sentence. Use 3 words from above.

Answers will vary.

Page 69

Word Problems

Compute

Each boat has one pair of oars. How many hands do you need to hold the oars?

4 boats = **8** oars = **8** hands

9 boats = **18** oars = **18** hands

2 boats = **4** oars = **4** hands

6 boats = **12** oars = **12** hands

It costs $5.00 an hour to rent a boat.

How much would it cost to rent a boat for 2 hours?

$ **10** for 2 hours

How much would it cost to rent a boat for 4 hours?

$ **20** for 4 hours

12 parents, 16 girls, and 22 boys rode to the lake on a bus.

How many people were there on the bus? **50**

How many feet? **100**

Page 70

Justify

Connections

Three of the words in each row belong together. Circle the word that does not belong. Then write to explain why the three items are alike.

1. heel   nail   arch   (stretch)
   The words are about a foot.

2. bend   kick   (drink)   jump
   The words are actions that legs can do.

3. ten   six   two   (five)
   The words are even numbers.

4. clip   (bend)   file   scrub
   The words are about cleaning fingernails.

5. grasp   write   (hop)   hold
   The words are actions that fingers can do.

Page 71

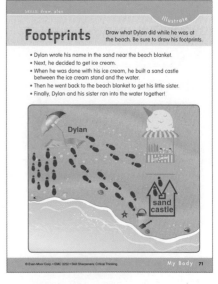

Illustrate

Footprints

Draw what Dylan did while he was at the beach. Be sure to draw his footprints.

• Dylan wrote his name in the sand near the beach blanket.
• Next, he decided to get ice cream.
• When he was done with his ice cream, he built a sand castle between the ice cream stand and the water.
• Then he went back to the beach blanket to get his little sister.
• Finally, Dylan and his sister ran into the water together!

Dylan

sand castle

Page 72

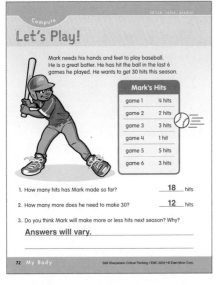

Let's Play!

Mark needs his hands and feet to play baseball. He is a great batter. He has hit the ball in the last 6 games he played. He wants to get 30 hits this season.

Mark's Hits	
game 1	4 hits
game 2	2 hits
game 3	3 hits
game 4	1 hit
game 5	5 hits
game 6	3 hits

1. How many hits has Mark made so far? **18** hits

2. How many more does he need to make 30? **12** hits

3. Do you think Mark will make more or less hits next season? Why?

Answers will vary.

My Body 72

Page 73

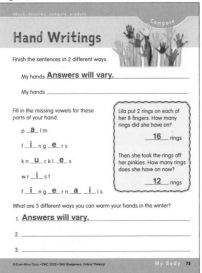

Hand Writings

Finish the sentences in 2 different ways.

My hands **Answers will vary.**

My hands

Fill in the missing vowels for these parts of your hand.

p **a** l m

f **i** ng **e** r s

kn **u** ckl **e** s

wr **i** s t

f **i** ng **e** rn **a** **i** ls

Lila put 2 rings on each of her 8 fingers. How many rings did she have on?

16 rings

Then she took the rings off her pinkies. How many rings does she have on now?

12 rings

What are 3 different ways you can warm your hands in the winter?

1. **Answers will vary.**

2.

3.

My Body 73

Page 75

Lost Shoes

Jill left her gym shoes somewhere. Help her find them. Draw a line to show Jill's path to her shoes.

start
classroom
gymnasium
library
music room
cafeteria
bus stop

My Body 75

Page 79

I Use These!

Write to tell how you use each thing.

pocket: **to hold things**

fork: **to eat with**

box: **to store things**

pencil: **to write with**

Put these things into 2 groups. Write the names in the boxes. Tell someone about the groups you made.

Group 1

Answers will vary.

Group 2

Things 79

Page 80

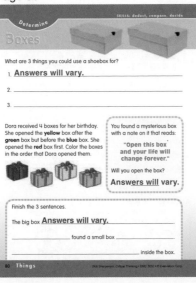

Boxes

What are 3 things you could use a shoebox for?

1. **Answers will vary.**

2.

3.

Dora received 4 boxes for her birthday. She opened the **yellow** box after the **green** box but before the **blue** box. She opened the **red** box first. Color the boxes in the order that Dora opened them.

You found a mysterious box with a note on it that reads:

"Open this box and your life will change forever."

Will you open the box?

Answers will vary.

Finish the 3 sentences.

The big box **Answers will vary.**

found a small box

inside the box.

Things 80

Page 81

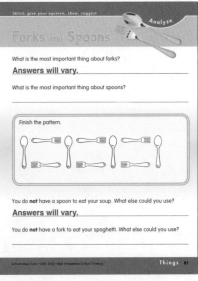

Forks and Spoons

What is the most important thing about forks?

Answers will vary.

What is the most important thing about spoons?

Finish the pattern.

You do **not** have a spoon to eat your soup. What else could you use?

Answers will vary.

You do **not** have a fork to eat your spaghetti. What else could you use?

Things 81

Page 82

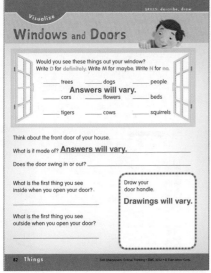

Windows and Doors

Would you see these things out your window? Write D for definitely. Write M for maybe. Write N for no.

trees ___ dogs ___ people
Answers will vary.
cars ___ flowers ___ beds
tigers ___ cows ___ squirrels

Think about the front door of your house.

What is it made of? **Answers will vary.**

Does the door swing in or out?

What is the first thing you see inside when you open your door?.

What is the first thing you see outside when you open your door?

Draw your door handle.

Drawings will vary.

Things 82

Page 84

Tools

Nail goes with **hammer** in the same way that **screw** goes with

screwdriver

Tools go with **toolshed** in the same way that **books** go with

bookshelf

Draw a line to match the tool to the word that describes what it does.

pound   measure   cut   turn   grip

You are building a birdhouse. List everything you will need.

1. **Answers will vary.**   4. **saw**

2. **wood**   5.

3. **nails**   6.

Things 84

Page 85

Hats

What are 3 reasons people wear hats?

1. **Answers will vary.**

2.

3.

What is wrong with this picture?

The girl has on a winter hat.

It is Silly Hat Day. Draw the silliest hat that you can!

Drawings will vary.

Why do you think some hats have brims?

Answers will vary.

Things 85

Answer Key 141

Tops

SKILLS: compare, infer, justify — Interpret

At Jamal's shirt shop, he sells only tops. Use the chart to answer the questions about what Jamal sold today.

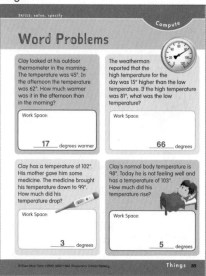

Bar chart showing: turtlenecks, collar shirts, tank tops, sweaters, vests, T-shirts (scale 0–30)

What did Jamal sell the most of? **tank tops**

How many T-shirts did he sell? **23**

Did he sell more sweaters or turtlenecks? **turtlenecks**

How many more tank tops than collar shirts did he sell? **7**

How many tops did he sell altogether? **107**

What do you think the weather was like at Jamal's shirt shop? Explain your answer.
The weather was probably warm because Jamal sold a lot of tank tops and T-shirts.

Analogies

Compare — SKILLS: infer, decide, determine

Analogies tell how one pair of things relates to another pair. Choose the correct word and write it on the line to complete each analogy.

1. **Bed** is to **sleeping** as **chair** is to **sitting** (table, sitting, wood)

2. **TV** is to **watching** as **book** is to **reading** (reading, words, story)

3. **Stove** is to **hot** as **freezer** is to **cold** (big, kitchen, cold)

4. **Tape** is to **sticky** as **rubber band** is to **stretchy** (stretchy, soft, long)

5. **Pillow** is to **soft** as **table** is to **hard** (wood, hard, dinner)

6. **Sink** is to **kitchen** as **tub** is to **bathroom** (water, bath, bathroom)

7. **Picture** is to **wall** as **curtain** is to **window** (window, mirror, fabric)

8. **Sponge** is to **washing** as **broom** is to **sweeping** (handle, brush, sweeping)

Word Problems

SKILLS: solve, specify — Compute

Clay looked at his outdoor thermometer in the morning. The temperature was 45°. In the afternoon the temperature was 62°. How much warmer was it in the afternoon than in the morning?

Work Space:
17 degrees warmer

The weatherman reported that the high temperature for the day was 15° higher than the low temperature. If the high temperature was 81°, what was the low temperature?

Work Space:
66 degrees

Clay has a temperature of 102°. His mother gave him some medicine. The medicine brought his temperature down to 99°. How much did his temperature drop?

Work Space:
3 degrees

Clay's normal body temperature is 98°. Today he is not feeling well and has a temperature of 103°. How much did his temperature rise?

Work Space:
5 degrees

I Like These!

SKILLS: give your opinion, classify, justify — Tell What You Know

Tell why you like each thing.

cookies: **Answers will vary.**

balloons: _____

music: _____

balls: _____

Put these things into 2 groups. Write the names in the boxes. Tell someone about the groups you made.

Group 1
Answers will vary.

Group 2

Balls

Conclude — SKILLS: solve, infer, order, draw

I am very heavy. I have 3 holes. What ball am I?
a bowling ball

I am brown. I am not round. What ball am I?
a football

I am orange. I am bouncy. What ball am I?
a basketball

Number the balls from 1 to 5 in order of size. The smallest ball should be 1.

5 beach ball
1 gum ball
3 baseball
4 soccer ball
2 golf ball

Which does not belong?

basketball   soccer ball   golf ball   playground ball

Why?
Answers will vary.

Draw the other half of each ball.

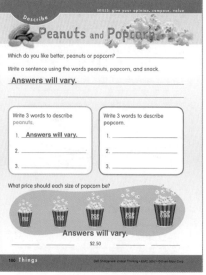

Music

Determine — SKILLS: draw, analyze, compare, contrast

What is one of the first songs you ever learned? **Answers will vary.**

How many songs do you think you know now? _____

What would you have if you combined a guitar and a trumpet? Draw it.
Drawings will vary.

Circle the symbol that does not belong.

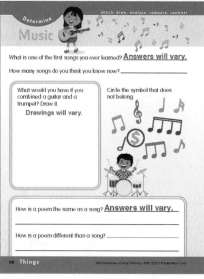

How is a poem the same as a song? **Answers will vary.**

How is a poem different than a song? _____

Crayons

SKILLS: classify, create — Show

Color these crayons with your 3 favorite colors.

Draw a picture. Use your 3 favorite colors.
Drawings will vary.

What do you think would happen to your crayons if you...

left them in the sun? **Answers will vary.**

dropped a book on them? _____

put them in water? _____

Finish the pattern.

Peanuts and Popcorn

Describe — SKILLS: give your opinion, compose, value

Which do you like better, peanuts or popcorn? _____

Write a sentence using the words peanuts, popcorn, and snack.
Answers will vary.

Write 3 words to describe peanuts.
1. **Answers will vary.**
2. _____
3. _____

Write 3 words to describe popcorn.
1. _____
2. _____
3. _____

What price should each size of popcorn be?

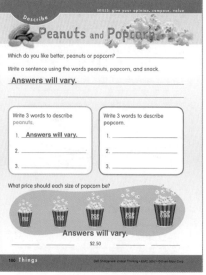

Answers will vary.
$2.50

Crazy About Crayons

SKILLS: analyze, show — Compare

Use this graph to compare the number of crayons the children have. Use one of these symbols in each box below.

> more than   < less than   = equal to

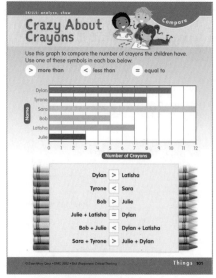

Bar graph: Dylan, Tyrone, Sara, Bob, Latisha, Julie — Number of Crayons 0–12

Dylan **>** Latisha

Tyrone **<** Sara

Bob **>** Julie

Julie + Latisha **=** Dylan

Bob + Julie **<** Dylan + Latisha

Sara + Tyrone **>** Julie + Dylan

Page 102

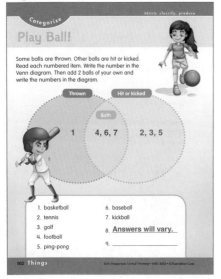

Categorize

Play Ball!

Some balls are thrown. Other balls are hit or kicked. Read each numbered item. Write the number in the Venn diagram. Then add 2 balls of your own and write the numbers in the diagram.

Thrown — Hit or kicked

Both

1 | 4, 6, 7 | 2, 3, 5

1. basketball
2. tennis
3. golf
4. football
5. ping-pong
6. baseball
7. kickball
8. **Answers will vary.**
9. _____

102 Things

Page 103

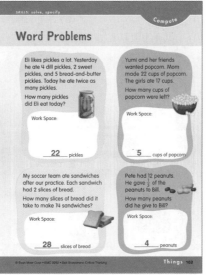

SKILLS: solve, specify

Word Problems

Compute

Eli likes pickles a lot. Yesterday he ate 4 dill pickles, 2 sweet pickles, and 5 bread-and-butter pickles. Today he ate twice as many pickles. How many pickles did Eli eat today?

Work Space:

22 pickles

Yumi and her friends wanted popcorn. Mom made 22 cups of popcorn. The girls ate 17 cups. How many cups of popcorn were left?

Work Space:

5 cups of popcorn

My soccer team ate sandwiches after our practice. Each sandwich had 2 slices of bread. How many slices of bread did it take to make 14 sandwiches?

Work Space:

28 slices of bread

Pete had 12 peanuts. He gave $\frac{1}{3}$ of the peanuts to Bill. How many peanuts did he give to Bill?

Work Space:

4 peanuts

Things 103

Page 104

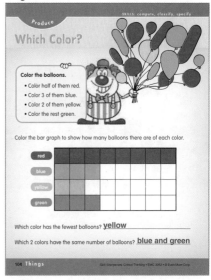

Produce

SKILLS: compute, classify, specify

Which Color?

Color the balloons.
- Color half of them red.
- Color 3 of them blue.
- Color 2 of them yellow.
- Color the rest green.

Color the bar graph to show how many balloons there are of each color.

red								
blue								
yellow								
green								

Which color has the fewest balloons? **yellow**

Which 2 colors have the same number of balloons? **blue and green**

104 Things

Page 105

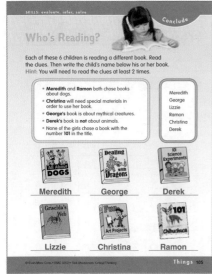

SKILLS: evaluate, infer, solve

Who's Reading?

Conclude

Each of these 6 children is reading a different book. Read the clues. Then write the child's name below his or her book.
Hint: You will need to read the clues at least 2 times.

- **Meredith** and **Ramon** both chose books about dogs.
- **Christina** will need special materials in order to use her book.
- **George's** book is about mythical creatures.
- **Derek's** book is **not** about animals.
- None of the girls chose a book with the number **101** in the title.

Meredith
George
Lizzie
Ramon
Christina
Derek

Meredith | **George** | **Derek**

Lizzie | **Christina** | **Ramon**

Things 105

Page 113

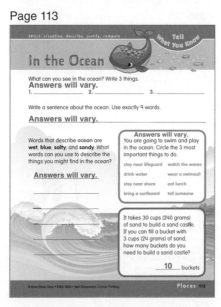

SKILLS: visualize, describe, justify, compute

In the Ocean

Tell What You Know

What can you see in the ocean? Write 3 things.
1. **Answers will vary.** 2. _____ 3. _____

Write a sentence about the ocean. Use exactly 9 words.

Answers will vary.

Words that describe ocean are **wet**, **blue**, **salty**, and **sandy**. What words can you use to describe the things you might find in the ocean?

Answers will vary.

_____

Answers will vary.
You are going to swim and play in the ocean. Circle the 3 most important things to do.

stay near lifeguard | watch the waves
drink water | wear a swimsuit
stay near shore | eat lunch
bring a surfboard | tell someone

It takes 30 cups (240 grams) of sand to build a sand castle. If you can fill a bucket with 3 cups (24 grams) of sand, how many buckets do you need to build a sand castle?

10 buckets

Places 113

Page 114

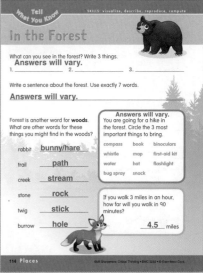

Tell What You Know

SKILLS: visualize, describe, reproduce, compute

In the Forest

What can you see in the forest? Write 3 things.
1. **Answers will vary.** 2. _____ 3. _____

Write a sentence about the forest. Use exactly 7 words.

Answers will vary.

Forest is another word for **woods**. What are other words for these things you might find in the woods?

rabbit	**bunny/hare**
trail	**path**
creek	**stream**
stone	**rock**
twig	**stick**
burrow	**hole**

Answers will vary.
You are going for a hike in the forest. Circle the 3 most important things to bring.

compass | book | binoculars
whistle | map | first-aid kit
water | hat | flashlight
bug spray | snack

If you walk 3 miles in an hour, how far will you walk in 90 minutes?

4.5 miles

114 Places

Page 115

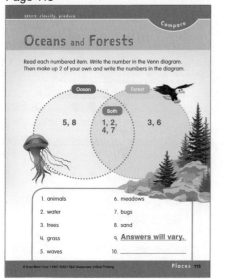

SKILLS: classify, produce

Oceans and Forests

Compare

Read each numbered item. Write the number in the Venn diagram. Then make up 2 of your own and write the numbers in the diagram.

Ocean — Forest

Both

5, 8 | 1, 2, 4, 7 | 3, 6

1. animals
2. water
3. trees
4. grass
5. waves
6. meadows
7. bugs
8. sand
9. **Answers will vary.**
10. _____

Places 115

Page 116

Produce

SKILLS: analyze, specify, illustrate

Under the Sea

Fish goes with scales in the same way that bear goes with

fur

Fish goes with fins in the same way that bird goes with

wings

Answers will vary.
Draw 2 straight lines to divide these fish into 3 groups of 3.

Read the words. Write the name of something that lives in the ocean.

very big **Answers will vary.**
very small _____
hard _____
moves quickly _____
has arms _____
people eat it _____

Draw Freddy Fish. He has:
- 3 fins
- a big tail
- spots

Drawings will vary.

115 Places

Page 117

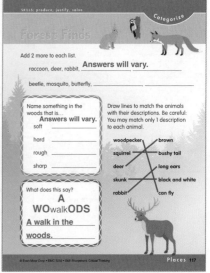

SKILLS: produce, justify, solve

Forest Finds

Categorize

Add 2 more to each list.

raccoon, deer, rabbit, **Answers will vary.**

beetle, mosquito, butterfly, _____

Name something in the woods that is...
Answers will vary.
soft _____
hard _____
rough _____
sharp _____

Draw lines to match the animals with their descriptions. Be careful! You may match only 1 description to each animal.

woodpecker — brown
squirrel — bushy tail
deer — long ears
skunk — black and white
rabbit — can fly

What does this say?

A WOwalkODS

A walk in the woods.

Places 117

© Evan-Moor Corp. • EMC 3252 • Skill Sharpeners: Critical Thinking

Answer Key 143

Page 118

Waves of 8

Color each box that contains a multiple of 8 to find the name of a fascinating ocean creature.

O	A	T	M	L
S	H	E	C	L
N	T	O	R	S
O	E	D	P	B
U	W	A	G	S

Draw a picture of this ocean creature. It should have **8** arms.

Drawing should be of an octopus.

118 Places

Page 119

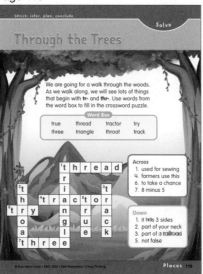

Through the Trees

We are going for a walk through the woods. As we walk along, we will see lots of things that begin with **tr-** and **thr-**. Use words from the word box to fill in the crossword puzzle.

Word Box
true · thread · tractor · try
three · triangle · throat · track

Across
1. used for sewing
4. farmers use this
6. to take a chance
7. 8 minus 5

Down
1. it has 3 sides
2. part of your neck
3. part of a railroad
5. not false

Crossword answers:
1. thread
2. throat
4. tractor
6. try
7. three

Places 119

Page 125

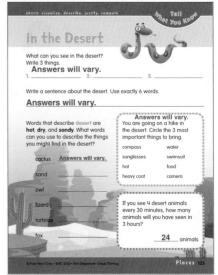

In the Desert

What can you see in the desert? Write 3 things.
1. **Answers will vary.** 2. 3.

Write a sentence about the desert. Use exactly 6 words.
Answers will vary.

Words that describe **desert** are **hot**, **dry**, and **sandy**. What words can you use to describe the things you might find in the desert?

cactus **Answers will vary.**
sand
owl
lizard
tortoise
fox

Answers will vary.
You are going on a hike in the desert. Circle the 3 most important things to bring.
compass · water
sunglasses · swimsuit
hat · food
heavy coat · camera

If you see 4 desert animals every 30 minutes, how many animals will you have seen in 3 hours?
24 animals

Places 125

Page 126

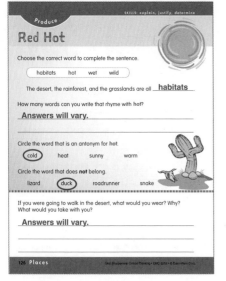

Red Hot

Choose the correct word to complete the sentence.
habitats · hot · wet · wild

The desert, the rainforest, and the grasslands are all **habitats**.

How many words can you write that rhyme with hot?
Answers will vary.

Circle the word that is an antonym for hot.
(cold) · heat · sunny · warm

Circle the word that does **not** belong.
lizard · (duck) · roadrunner · snake

If you were going to walk in the desert, what would you wear? Why? What would you take with you?
Answers will vary.

126 Places

Page 129

Word Problems

Jakob went for a walk with Grandpa. They left home at 11 o'clock. "Be back in 4 hours," said Jakob's mother.
At what time did they have to be back?
Show your answer on the clock.

3 o'clock

Jakob likes to go on walks with Grandpa. Last month they walked on 9 days. This month they walked on 8 days.

On how many days did they walk in the last 2 months? **17** days

How many days do you think they will walk next month? _____ days
Tell why.
Answers will vary.

Places 129

Page 130

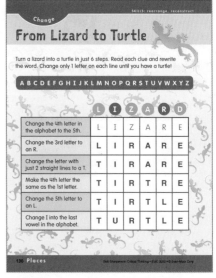

From Lizard to Turtle

Turn a lizard into a turtle in just 6 steps. Read each clue and rewrite the word. Change only 1 letter on each line until you have a turtle!

A B C D E F G H I J K L M N O P Q R S T U V W X Y Z

L I Z A R D

Clue						
Change the 4th letter in the alphabet to the 5th.	L	I	Z	A	R	E
Change the 3rd letter to an R.	L	I	R	A	R	E
Change the letter with just 2 straight lines to a T.	T	I	R	A	R	E
Make the 4th letter the same as the 1st letter.	T	I	R	T	R	E
Change the 5th letter to an L.	T	I	R	T	L	E
Change I into the last vowel in the alphabet.	T	U	R	T	L	E

130 Places

Page 131

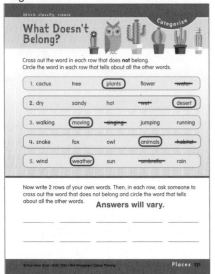

What Doesn't Belong?

Cross out the word in each row that does **not** belong. Circle the word in each row that tells about all the other words.

1. cactus · tree · (plants) · flower · ~~water~~
2. dry · sandy · hot · ~~wet~~ · (desert)
3. walking · (moving) · ~~singing~~ · jumping · running
4. snake · fox · owl · (animals) · ~~habitat~~
5. wind · (weather) · sun · ~~umbrella~~ · rain

Now write 2 rows of your own words. Then, in each row, ask someone to cross out the word that does not belong and circle the word that tells about all the other words. **Answers will vary.**

131 Places

Page 132

Desert Words

Find the desert words. Circle each one. Cross off the word from the list.

B	X	N	M	L	K	F	O	X
Z	P	I	H	Q	J	I	R	L
W	O	T	A	C	H	G	D	I
G	Q	A	H	A	C	F	E	Z
E	W	C	A	C	T	U	S	A
S	L	A	B	E	S	R	E	R
M	K	B	I	Z	A	D	R	D
T	R	F	T	D	R	Y	T	V
Z	S	G	A	P	S	E	L	O
Q	X	R	T	H	O	T	Y	X

Word Box
CACTUS · LIZARD
DESERT · HABITAT
OWL · DRY
FOX · HOT

132 Places

Page 133

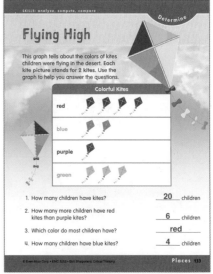

Flying High

This graph tells about the colors of kites children were flying in the desert. Each kite picture stands for 2 kites. Use the graph to help you answer the questions.

Colorful Kites
red
blue
purple
green

1. How many children have kites? **20** children
2. How many more children have red kites than purple kites? **6** children
3. Which color do most children have? **red**
4. How many children have blue kites? **4** children

133 Places

---

144 Answer Key